D1329725

GOLDEN BOY

BY
CLIFFORD ODETS

★

★

DRAMATISTS
PLAY SERVICE
INC.

Golden Boy was first presented by the Group Theatre at the Belasco Theatre on the evening of November 4th, 1937, with the following members of the Group Theatre Acting Company:

(In order of speech)

Tom Moody	Roman Bohnen
Lorna Moon	Frances Farmer
Joe Bonaparte	Luther Adler
Tokio	Art Smith
Mr. Carp	Lee J. Cobb
Siggie	Jules Garfield
Mr. Bonaparte	Morris Carnovsky
Anna	Phoebe Brand
Frank Bonaparte	John O'Malley
Roxy Gottlieb	Robert Lewis
Eddie Fuseli	Elia Kazan
Pepper White	Harry Bratsburg
Mickey	Michael Gordon
Call Boy	Bert Conway
Sam	Martin Ritt
Lewis	Charles Crisp
Drake	Howard Da Silva
Driscoll	Charles Niemeyer
Barker	Karl Malden

Direction by Harold Clurman
Settings by Mordecai Gorelik

(Some non-speaking extras are called for in the text and a number of these can be somewhat increased or decreased.)

SCENES

Act I

Scene 1. The office of Tom Moody. Scene 2. The Bonaparte home. That night. Scene 3. The office. Two months later. Scene 4. A park bench. A few nights later. Scene 5. The Bonaparte home. Midnight, six weeks later.

Act II

Scene 1. A gymnasium. Five months later. Scene 2. The park bench. A few nights later. Scene 3. The office. The following day. Scene 4. A dressing room in the Arena. Six weeks later.

Act III

Scene 1. The office. Six months later. Scene 2. The dressing room. The following night. Scene 3. The Bonaparte home. Several hours later.

For scene designs, see page 82.

3

PRODUCTION NOTES

The present edition of *Golden Boy* was authorized by Mr. Odets, who permitted us to clarify, for the benefit of nonprofessional producers, some of the stage directions, and to prepare, under his supervision, a simple plan which will enable any producing group to mount the play in a single and very simple unit set. The play calls for five different sets, but each one can be easily suggested by a very few articles of furniture which are indicated in the text. On page 82, will be found five simple line-cut stage diagrams showing the basic necessary articles of furniture, and their approximate positions. The background for each set can be of the simplest, consisting either of curtains or a few more or less nondescript flats or parts of flats. As a matter of fact, the setting should, in no case, be too realistic.

Certain sound effects called for in the stage directions are, of course, extremely simple, and can be devised by any director. Other effects will perhaps be more easily suggested by sound effect records. A list of these will be found on the copyright page of the present volume. These can all be ordered through Dramatists Play Service.

GOLDEN BOY

ACT I

SCENE 1

The small Broadway office of TOM MOODY, *the fight manager.*[1]

The office is scantily furnished, contains desk, chairs, telephone (on desk) and couch. With MOODY *at present is his girl,* LORNA MOON. *There is a certain quiet glitter about this girl, and if she is sometimes hard, it is more from necessity than choice. Her eyes often hold a soft, sad glance. Likewise,* MOODY'S *explosiveness covers a soft, boyish quality, and at the same time he possesses a certain vulnerable quality which women find very attractive.*

The time is eighteen months ago.

As the lights fade in, we catch these two at the height of one of their frequent fights.

MOODY. Pack up your clothes and go! Go! Who the hell's stopping you?

LORNA. You mean it?

MOODY. You brought up the point yourself.

LORNA. No, I didn't!

MOODY. Didn't you say you had a good mind to leave me?

LORNA. No, I said ——

MOODY. You said you were going to pack!

LORNA. I said I feel like a tramp and I don't like it. I want to get married, I want ——

MOODY. Go home, Lorna, go home! I ain't got time to discuss it. Gimme some air. It's enough I got my wife on my neck.

LORNA. What does she say?

[1] Production Notes, p. 4.

MOODY. Who?

LORNA. Your wife—your sweet Goddam Monica!

MOODY. She wants five thousand dollars to give me the divorce. (LORNA *laughs*.) I don't see that it's funny.

LORNA. Look, Tom, this means as much to me as it does to you. If she's out of the way, we can get married. Otherwise I'm a tramp from Newark. I don't like the feeling.

MOODY. Lorna, for pete's sake, use your noodle! When I get rid of Monica, we'll marry. Now, do I have to bang you on the nose to make you understand?

LORNA. Go to hell! . . . But come back tonight. (MOODY's *answer is to look at her, then smile, then walk to her. They kiss.*)

MOODY. If I had the money, I'd buy you something—I don't know what—a big ostrich feather! If Kaplan wins tonight, I'll take you dancing at the Park.

LORNA. He won't win.

MOODY. How do you know? I don't know—how do *you* know?

LORNA. Are you crazy? Do you think your Mr. Kaplan can go ten rounds with the Baltimore Chocolate Drop?

MOODY. How do I know?

LORNA. It's the Twentieth Century, Tom—no more miracles. (MOODY's *face turns worried.* LORNA *smiles.*) You know what I like about you—you take everything so serious.

MOODY. Who will if I don't? I've been off the gold standard for eight years. This used to be a gorgeous town. New York was hot with money. Kaplan gets four hundred bucks tonight. In the old days, that was nothing. Those were the days when I had Marty Welch, the heavyweight contender—Cy Webster, who got himself killed in a big, red Stutz. In '27 and 8 you couldn't go to sleep— the town was crawling with attractions. . . .

LORNA. My mother died in '28.

MOODY. I haven't had a break in years. " Carry me back to old Virginny "—that's how I feel. There isn't much of a future. (*Suddenly despondent,* MOODY *goes back to his desk.*)

LORNA. I was fooling.

MOODY. What about?

LORNA. Do you think I'd leave you?

MOODY. Why not? I'm an old man. What can I give you?

LORNA. A bang on the nose for a start. But what can I give you?

6

MOODY. A boy who can fight. Find me a good black boy and I'll show you a mint.

LORNA. Are good boys so hard to find?

MOODY. Honest to God, you make me sick to my stomach! What do you think I took a trip to Philadelphia? What do you think I went to Chicago? Wasn't I up in Boston for a week? You think good boys are laying around like pop-corn? I'd even take a bantamweight, if I found one.

LORNA. How about a nice lady fighter with a beard —— (*Preparing to leave.*) Well, I'll see you tonight, Moody.

MOODY. (*Thoughtfully.*) I'd give me right eye for a good black boy.

LORNA. Let me have your right eye for a minute. (*She kisses his eye.* MOODY *begins to embrace her—she eludes his grasp.*) That's to keep you hot. But if the truth were known—" yours till hell freezes over."

MOODY. I need you, I need you, Lorna—I need you all the time. I'd like to give you everything you want. Push your mouth over. . . . (LORNA *holds her face to his, he kisses her. Suddenly a youth is standing at office door.* LORNA *sees him and breaks away.*)

BOY. (*Entering, breathing quickly.*) Mr. Moody . . .

MOODY. (*Spinning around.*) Don't you knock when you come in an office?

BOY. Sometimes I knock, sometimes I don't.

MOODY. Say your piece and get the hell out!

BOY. I just ran over from the gym . . .

MOODY. What gym?

BOY. Where Kaplan trains. He just broke his hand. . . .(MOODY *stiffens to attention.*) It's a fact.

MOODY. (*Grasping phone.*) Is Tokio over there? My trainer?

BOY. He's looking after Kaplan. (MOODY *begins to dial phone but abruptly changes his mind and replaces phone.*)

MOODY. You can put me in the bug-house right now. Moody is the name, folks—step right up and wipe your shoes! Ah, that Kaplan! That phonus bolonus! (*He sits at his desk in despair.*) Now I have to call up Roxy Gottlieb and cancel the match. His club's in the red as it is.

BOY. I don't think it's necessary to cancel, Tom.

MOODY. (*Aware of the boy for the first time.*) Oh, you don't?

7

Who the hell are you? And who the hell are you to call me Tom? Are we acquainted?

BOY. I wrote you a couple of letters. I can do that stretch.

MOODY. What stretch?

BOY. Why don't you let me take Kaplan's place tonight?

MOODY. (*Sarcastically.*) Go slow and tell me again. . . . What?

BOY. (*Coolly.*) I can take Kaplan's place. . . .

MOODY. You mean you want to fight the Baltimore Chocolate Drop? *You.* (*The* BOY *remains silent.* MOODY *comes out from behind his desk and stands face to face with the* BOY. *With sudden discovery.*) You're cock-eyed too.

BOY. (*Quietly.*) Can't you fix it up with Roxy Gottlieb?

MOODY. (*Suddenly.*) Looka, kid, go home, kid, before I blame Kaplan's glass mitts on *you.* Then you won't like it, and I won't like it, and Miss Moon here, she won't like it.

BOY. (*Turning to* LORNA.) How do you do, Miss Moon. (LORNA *smiles at the* BOY'S *quiet confidence.*) I need a good manager, Mr. Moody. You used to be tops around town—everyone says so. I think you can develop me. I can fight. You don't know it, but I can fight. Kaplan's been through for years. He may be the best fighter in your stable, but he's a stumble-bum for the younger boys growing up. Why don't you give me this chance, Tom?

MOODY. I don't want you calling me Tom! (*He glares at the* BOY *and then returns to desk and telephone.*)

BOY. I'm waiting for your answer. (MOODY'S *answer is an exasperated glance as he begins to dial phone. The* BOY *half approaches desk.*) There are forty-three thousand minutes in a month—can't you give me five?

MOODY. I'll give you this phone in the head in a minute! Who are you? What the hell do you want? Where do you fight?

BOY. (*With cool persistence.*) We ought to get together, Tom.

MOODY. I don't want you calling me Tom. You're brash, you're fresh, you're callow—and you're cock-eyed! In fact, you're an insult to my whole nature! Now get out! (MOODY *turns back to phone and begins dialing again. The* BOY *stands there, poised on his toes, not sure of his next move. He turns and looks at* LORNA. *She nods her head and gives him a faint smile of encouragement. On phone.*) This is Tom Moody. . . . Is Tokio there? . . . (*He hangs up phone and holds the instrument thoughtfully.*) Tokio's on his way over.

8

BOY. The Baltimore Chocolate Drop is not as good as you think he is. (MOODY *suddenly whirls around and holds phone high over his head in a threatening gesture. The* BOY *steps back lightly and continues.*) I've studied his style for months; I've perfected the exact punch to quench his thirst. Did you ever watch closely? (*Acting it out.*) He likes to pull your lead—he hesitates for a second—he pulls your lead—he slips his face away and then he's in. Suppose you catch that second when he hesitates—he's open for the punch!

MOODY. (*Sarcastically.*) And what do you do with his left hook?

BOY. (*Simply.*) Avoid it.

MOODY. (*Lowering phone.*) Looka, you idiot, did you ever hear of Phil Mateo?

BOY. I heard of him.

MOODY. The Chocolate Drop marked him lousy in twelve minutes and ten seconds. Was Kid Peters within your ken? And did you ever hear of Eddie Newton? The Chocolate gave him the blues in two rounds. And Frisco Samuels and Mike Mason . . .

BOY. Did you ever hear of me?

MOODY. (*Sarcastically.*) No, who are you? I would honestly like to know—who are you?

BOY. (*Quietly.*) My name is Bonaparte. (MOODY *howls with laughter, and even* LORNA, *sympathetic to the* BOY, *laughs. The* BOY *continues.*) I don't think it's funny. . . .

MOODY. Didn't that name used to get you a little giggle in school? Tell the truth, Bonaparte. Didn't it?

BOY. Call me Joe.

MOODY. (*Laughing.*) And your eyes. . . . Didn't they used to get a little giggle too?

JOE. You don't seem as intelligent as I thought you were.

LORNA. (*To the laughing* MOODY, *seeing the* BOY'S *pain.*) Stop it, Tom.

MOODY. (*Laughing.*) You can't blame me, Bonaparte. . . . I haven't laughed for years.

JOE. I don't like it. . . . I don't want you to do it. (*Suddenly* JOE *grabs* MOODY *by the coat lapels.* MOODY, *surprised, shakes him off. At the same time a small, quiet man enters office. He is* TOKIO, MOODY'S *trainer.*) I'm sorry I did that, Tom. We ought to be together, Tom—not apart.

MOODY. Tokio, did you send this kid here?

9

TOKIO. No.

MOODY. Take him out before I brain him! (*He storms back to his desk.*)

TOKIO. (*After looking at the* BOY.) You hear about Kaplan?

MOODY. This idiot told me. It's the end of everything! I'm off my top with the whole thing! Kaplan was our meal-ticket. I'm up to the throat in scandal, blackmail, perjury, alimony and all points west!

TOKIO. (*Turning to* JOE.) You oughta be ashamed to show your face in this office.

JOE. If Kaplan's mother fed him milk, he wouldn't have those brittle bones.

MOODY. ? ? ? ?

TOKIO. (*To* MOODY.) This is the boy who did it to Kaplan.

MOODY. ? ? ?

TOKIO. I went down for an apple and I came back and Kaplan's sparring with this kid—picked him up in the gym. The next thing I know, Kaplan's down on the floor with a busted mitt.

JOE. (*Modestly.*) I took it on the elbow.

MOODY. ! ! (*Silence finally.*)

LORNA. Where do you come from, Bonaparte?

JOE. Here.

LORNA. How old are you?

JOE. Twenty-one—tomorrow.

MOODY. (*After a look at* LORNA.) Fight much?

JOE. Enough.

MOODY. Where?

JOE. (*Fabricating.*) Albany, Syracuse . . .

LORNA. Does Roxy Gottlieb know you?

JOE. I never fought at his club.

MOODY. (*Harshly.*) Does he know you?

JOE. No. (TOKIO *and* MOODY *look at each other. Phone rings.*)

MOODY. (*On the phone.*) Hello. . . . " What's this you hear? " . . . You hear the truth, Roxy. . . . He bust his mitt again. . . . I can't help it if you got *fifty* judgments on your club. . . . The same to you. . . . Your mother too! (*Keeping his eyes on* BONA-PARTE.) If you tie up your big flabby mouth for a minute, I'll give you some news. I'm in a position to do you a big favor. I got a replacement—*better* than Kaplan . . . Bonaparte. . . . No,

10

Bon-a-parte. (*Holds hand over mouthpiece and asks* BOY.) Is that crap?

JOE. No, that's my name.

MOODY. (*Back at phone.*) That's right, like in Napoleon. . . . (*Looks the* BOY *over appraisingly.*) One hundred and thirty . . .

JOE. Three.

MOODY. Hundred and thirty-three. Your customers'll eat him up. I'll bring him right over . . . you can take my word—the kid's a cock-eyed wonder . . . *your* mother too! (*He bangs up and turns around.* JOE *is the focus of all eyes.*) It's revenge on somebody—maybe God.

JOE. (*Quietly.*) I think you'll be surprised.

MOODY. (*Sadly.*) Do your worst, kid. I've been surprised by experts.

JOE. Don't worry, Tom.

MOODY. Call me Tom again and I'll break your neck!!

QUICK FADEOUT

ACT I

SCENE 2

Later that night.

The combination dining and front room of the Bonaparte home.[1] *A round dining-room table, littered with newspapers, is lighted from directly above like a billiard table. Plaster busts of Mozart and Beethoven are on the sideboard. A cage of love birds at the other side of the room.*[2] *Sitting at the table are two men:* MR. BONAPARTE, *the father of* JOE, *and a Jewish friend, a* MR. CARP, *who owns the local candy and stationery store.*

As the lights fade in, MR. BONAPARTE *turns his newspaper.* MR. CARP *is slowly pouring beer from a bottle. He begins to sip it as* SIGGIE, MR. BONAPARTE'S *son-in-law, enters from kitchen (door* L.). *He is barefooted, dressed in an undershirt, trousers and hung-down sus-*

[1] See Production Notes, p. 4.
[2] Optional.

11

penders. He brings his own beer and glass, which he begins to fill with an expert's eye. In the silence, MR. CARP takes a long, cool sip of beer combined with a murmur of relish.

CARP. (*Finally.*) I don't take it easy. That's my trouble—if I could only learn to take it easy . . .

SIGGIE. What do you call it now, what you're doing?

CARP. Say, it's after business hours.

SIGGIE. That's a business? A man who runs a candy store is an outcast of the world. Don't even sell *nickel* candies—*penny* candies!

CARP. And your taxicab business makes you higher in the social scale?

SIGGIE. So I'm an outcast too. Don't change the subject. Like my father-in-law here—he's always changing the subject when I get a little practical on him. (*Putting his beer on table and scratching himself under the arms like a monkey.*) You—I'm talking about you, Mr. Bonaparte.

BONAPARTE. (*Suddenly shooting out two words.*) Ha ha! (*He then resumes his reading.*)

SIGGIE. Every time I talk money, he gives me that horse laugh. Suppose you bought me a cab—I could pay it off by the week.

BONAPARTE. (*Who talks with an Italian accent.*) I don't go in taxicab business.

SIGGIE. I am married to your daughter and when you do this little thing, you do it for her and me together. A cab in two shifts is a big source of profit. Joe takes the night shift. I'm a married man so you don't expect me to take the night shift. (ANNA, SIGGIE'S *wife, in a nightgown, pokes her head in at door.*)

ANNA. Come to bed, Siggie. You'll wake up the whole neighborhood. (ANNA *disappears.*)

SIGGIE. See? I'm a married man! You don't expect me to take the night shift.

BONAPARTE. (*Having heard his talk for months.*) No, Siggie . . . no.

SIGGIE. No, what?

BONAPARTE. No taxicab.

SIGGIE. Don't you wanna help your own family, Foolish? After all, Joe's your own son—he's a man, no kid no more ——

12

BONAPARTE. Tomorrow's twenty-one.

SIGGIE. If he don't work he'll turn into a real bum. Look how late he's staying out at night.

BONAPARTE. I don't expects for Joe to drive taxi.

SIGGIE. He's got to do something. He can drive like a fire engine. Why not?

BONAPARTE. He gonna do something.

SIGGIE. What? Play his violinsky in the backyards?

ANNA. (*Looking in at door again.*) Come to bed, Siggie! Poppa, don't talk to him so he'll come to bed! (ANNA *disappears again.*)

SIGGIE. (*Annoyed.*) Women! Always buzzing around. (BONAPARTE'S *only answer is to turn over newspaper on table before him.*)

CARP. (*Reflectively.*) Women . . . the less we have to do with women the better. As Schopenhauer says, " Much ado about nothing . . . the comedy of reproduction." (*He wags his head bitterly.*) Women . . . !

SIGGIE. I'm hungry, but I ain't got the heart to go in the kitchen again. It reminds me of how my wife slaves for this family of crazy wops! A fine future for an intelligent woman!

BONAPARTE. She'sa your wife, but also my daughter. She'sa not so intelligent as you say. Also, you are not so intelligent!

SIGGIE. You can't insult me, I'm too ignorant! (ANNA *now comes fully into the room. She is buxom, energetic, good-natured and adenoidal.*)

ANNA. Poppa, why don't you let Siggie come to bed? Looka him, walking around barefooted!

BONAPARTE. I don't stop him. . . .

SIGGIE. Sure he stops me—he stops me every night. I'm worried. I don't sleep. It's my Jewish disposition. He don't wanna help me out, your old man. He wants me to drive a company cab and submit to the brutalities of the foremen all my life. I could be in a healthy little enterprise for myself, but your old man don't wanna help me out.

ANNA. Why don't you buy Siggie a cab, poppa? You got the cash.

SIGGIE. Buy it for Siggie and Joe.

ANNA. For Siggie and Joe—it don't have to be a new one.

SIGGIE. (*After giving his wife a stabbing glance.*) Sure, even an old one—the way they recondition them now-a-days ——

BONAPARTE. Children, gone to bed.

SIGGIE. Don't tell a lie—how much you got in the bank?
BONAPARTE. (*With a smile.*) Millions.
SIGGIE. Four thousand?
BONAPARTE. No.
SIGGIE. Three? (BONAPARTE *shakes his head.*) Three? . . .
ANNA. What's your business how much he's got?
SIGGIE. Shut up, Duchess! Am I asking for my health? If I wanna take you out of the kitchen, is that the gratitude I get? You and your father, you get my goat! I'm sore!
ANNA. Come to bed, Siggie.
SIGGIE. " Come to bed, come to bed!" What the hell's so special in bed? (ANNA'S *answer is a warm prolonged giggle.*) It's a conspiracy around here to put me to bed. I'm warning one thing: if matters go from worse to worse, don't ever expect me to support this family, I'm warning!
BONAPARTE. (*Smiling kindly.*) We have-a receive the warning. We are in a conspiracy against you—go to bed. (*He turns back to his newspaper.* SIGGIE *sees he has lost again and now turns on his wife.*)
SIGGIE. Who asked you to stick in your two cents about second-hand cabs? As long as I'm not gonna get it, I'll tell you what I want—a first-class job, fresh from the factory. (*He suddenly swats her on the head with a rolled-up newspaper. She hits him back. He returns her blow.*)
ANNA. Don't be so free with your hands! (*He hits her again. She hits him back.*) You got some nerve, Siggie!
SIGGIE. (*Hitting her again.*) The next time I'll break your neck— I'm super-disgusted with you!
BONAPARTE. (*Standing up.*) Stop this . . .
SIGGIE. (*Turning to him.*) And with you, I'm super-finished! (*Turning back to his wife.*) Sit out here with this Unholy Alliance —I'll sleep alone tonight. (*He starts for door.* BONAPARTE *puts his arm around* ANNA *who begins to sob.*)
BONAPARTE. Hit your wife in private, not in public!
CARP. A man hits his wife and it is the first step to fascism!
SIGGIE. (*To* CARP.) What are you talking about, my little prince! I love my wife. You don't stop talking how you hate yours. (*Now to* BONAPARTE.) And as for you, don't make believe you care!—Do I have to fall on my knees to you otherwise? We wanna raise a family—it's a normal instinct. Take your arm off her.

14

ANNA. (*Suddenly moving over to* SIGGIE.) That's right, poppa. He can hit me any time he likes.

SIGGIE. (*His arm around her.*) And we don't want you interfering in our affairs unless you do it the right way!

ANNA. That's right, poppa—you mind your g.d. business! (BONAPARTE, *repressing a smile, slowly sits.*)

SIGGIE. In the bed, Duchess.

ANNA. (*With a giggle.*) Good night.

BONAPARTE and CARP. Good night. (*She exits. After a belligerent look at the pair at table,* SIGGIE *follows her.*)

BONAPARTE. (*Bursting into hushed laughter.*) There'sa olda remark—never interfere in the laws of nature and you gonna be happy. Love! Ha, ha!

CARP. (*Gloomily.*) Happy? A famous man remarked in the last century, "Pleasure is negative."

BONAPARTE. I feela good. Like-a to have some music! Hey, where'sa my boy, Joe? (*Looks at his watch, is surprised.*) One o'clock . . . don't come home yet. Hey, he make'a me worry!

CARP. You think you got worries? Wait, you're a young man yet. You got a son, Joe. He practised on his fiddle for ten years? He won a gold medal, the best in the city? They gave him a scholarship in the Erickson Institute? Tomorrow he's twenty-one, yeah?

BONAPARTE. (*Emphatically.*) Yeah!

CARP. (*Leaning forward and dramatically making his point.*) Suppose a war comes? Before you know it, he's in the army!

BONAPARTE. Naw, naw! Whata you say! Naw!

CARP. (*Wagging his head in imitation.*) Look in the papers! On every side the clouds of war ——

BONAPARTE. My Joe gotta biga talent. Yesterday I buy-a him present! (*With a dramatic flourish he brings a violin case out of the bottom part of sideboard.*)

CARP. (*As the case is opened.*) It looks like a coffin for a baby.

BONAPARTE. (*Looking down at violin in its case.*) His teacher help me to picka him.

CARP. (*The connoisseur.*) Fine, fine—beautiful, fine! A cultural thing!

BONAPARTE. (*Touching it fondly.*) The mosta golden present for his birthday which I give him tonight.

CARP. How much, if I'm not getting too personal, did such a violin cost you?

BONAPARTE. Twelve hundred dollars.

CARP. (*Shocked.*) What?

BONAPARTE. You're surprised of me? Well, I waita for this moment many years.

CARP. (*Sitting.*) Ask yourself a pertinent remark: could a boy make a living playing this instrument in our competitive civilization today?

BONAPARTE. Why? Don't expect for Joe to be a millionaire. He don't need it, to be millionaire. A good life'sa possible ——

CARP. For men like us, yes. But nowadays is it possible for a young man to give himself to the Muses? Could the Muses put bread and butter on the table?

BONAPARTE. No millionaire is necessary. Joe love music. Music is the great cheer-up in the language of all countries. I learn that from Joe. (CARP *sighs as* BONAPARTE *replaces violin in buffet.*)

CARP. But in the end, as Schopenhauer says, what's the use to try something? For every wish we get, ten remains unsatisfied. Death is playing with us as a cat and her mouse!

BONAPARTE. You make-a me laugh, Mr. Carp. You say life'sa bad. No, life'sa good. Siggie and Anna fight—good! They love—good! You say life'sa bad . . . Well, is pleasure for you to say so. No? The streets, winter a' summer—trees, cats—I love-a them all. The gooda boys and girls, they who sing and whistle—(*Bursts into a moment of gay whistling*)—very good! The eating and sleeping, drinking wine—very good! I gone around on my wagon and talk to many people—nice! Howa you like the big buildings of the city?

CARP. Buildings? And suppose it falls? A house fell down last week on Staten Island!

BONAPARTE. Ha ha, you make me laugh, ha ha! (*Now enters* FRANK BONAPARTE, *oldest son of the family, simple, intelligent, observant.*) Hello, Frank.

FRANK. Hello, poppa . . . Mr. Carp . . .

CARP. (*Nodding.*) What's new in the world?

FRANK. (*Dropping newspapers to table, but keeping one for himself.*) Read 'em and weep. March first tomorrow—spring on the way. Flowers soon budding, birds twittering—south wind . . . Cannons, bombs and airplane raids! Where's Joe? Did you give him the fiddle yet?

BONAPARTE. No, not in yet. Siggie and Anna sleep. Hungry?

FRANK. (*Beginning to undress—putting his coat on the back of a chair.*) No, I'm tired. I'll see you in the morning, before I leave.

CARP. Going away again?

FRANK. South. Tex-tiles. There's hell down there in textiles (*He sits in chair on the other side of the room and looks at a paper.*)

CARP. I don't begin to understand it—tex-tiles! What's it his business if the workers in tex-tiles don't make good wages!

BONAPARTE. Frank, he fighta for eat, for good life. Why not!

CARP. Foolish!

BONAPARTE. What ever you got ina your nature to do isa not foolish!

CARP. (*Flipping over newspaper.*) For instance—look: playing baseball isn't foolish?

BONAPARTE. No, if you like-a to do.

CARP. Look! Four or five pages—baseball—tennisball—it gives you an idea what a civilization! You ever seen a baseball game?

BONAPARTE. No.

CARP. (*Wagging his head.*) Hit a ball, catch a ball . . . believe me, my friend—nonsense!

FRANK. Poppa, where did you say Joe was?

BONAPARTE. Don't know ——

FRANK. Poppa, you better brace yourself in your chair!

BONAPARTE. What? (FRANK *places paper before* BONAPARTE. *He reads aloud.*)

FRANK. Looka this, Joe's had a fight. " Flash: Chocolate Drop fails to K.O. new cock-eyed wonder." Take a look at the picture.

CARP. What?

BONAPARTE. What?

FRANK. It's my little brother Joie, or I don't know a scab from a picket!

BONAPARTE. Had a fight? That is foolish—not possible.

FRANK. (*Pointing with his finger.*) There's his name—Bonaparte.

BONAPARTE. (*Puzzled.*) Musta be some other boy. (FRANK *suddenly flips over newspaper. The others immediately see the reason:* JOE *stands in the door, in the shadows.*)

JOE. (*In the shadows.*) Gee, you're up late. . . .

BONAPARTE. We waita for you. (JOE *slowly moves into the light. His face is bruised and over one eye is a piece of adhesive tape.*)

JOE. (*Seeing their looks.*) I had a fight—a boy in the park ——

BONAPARTE. He hit you?

17

JOE. I hit him.

BONAPARTE. You hurt?

JOE. No. (BONAPARTE *casts a furtive look in the direction of the other men.*)

BONAPARTE. Whata you fight him for?

JOE. Didn't like what he said to me.

BONAPARTE. What he said?

JOE. (*Evasively.*) It's a long story and I'm tired.

BONAPARTE. (*Trying to break a pause of embarrassment.*) I was say to Mr. Carp tomorrow is your birthday. How you like to be so old?

JOE. I forgot about that! I mean I forgot for the last few hours. Where do you think I was? Do you want the truth?

FRANK. Truth is cheap. We bought it for two cents. (*He turns over paper and shows* JOE *his own face.* JOE *looks at picture, likes it. General silence.*)

JOE. (*Finally, belligerently.*) Well, what are you going to do about it?

BONAPARTE. (*Still puzzled.*) Abouta what?

JOE. (*Challengingly.*) Tomorrow's my birthday!

FRANK. What's that got to do with being a gladiator?

JOE. (*Turning to* FRANK, *with sudden vehemence.*) Mind your business! You don't know me—I see you once a year; what do you know about me?

FRANK. (*Smiling.*) You're a dumb kid!

BONAPARTE. (*Starting to his feet.*) Hey, waita one-a minute. What'sa for this excite-a-ment?

JOE. (*Hotly.*) I don't want to be criticized! Nobody takes me serious here! I want to do what I want. I proved it tonight I'm good—I went out to earn some money and I earned! I had a professional fight tonight—maybe I'll have some more.

CARP. You honest to God had a fight?

JOE. (*Glaring at* CARP.) Why not?

FRANK. (*To* JOE.) No one's criticizin'.

BONAPARTE. That's right.

JOE. (*Half sheepishly.*) I don't know why I got so sore. . . .

FRANK. You're expecting opposition all the time ——

BONAPARTE. Sit down, Joe—resta you'self.

JOE. Don't want to sit. Every birthday I ever had I sat around. Now'sa time for standing. Poppa, I have to tell you—I don't like myself, past, present and future. Do you know there are men who have wonderful things from life? Do you think they're better than me? Do you think I like this feeling of no possessions? Of learning about the world from Carp's encyclopedia? Frank don't know what it means—he travels around, sees the world! (*Turning to* FRANK.) You don't know what it means to sit around here and watch the months go ticking by! Do you think that's a life for a boy my age? Tomorrow's my birthday! I change my life!

BONAPARTE. Justa like that?

JOE. Just like that!

FRANK. And what do you do with music?

JOE. Who says I'm married to music? I take a vacation—the notes won't run away!

FRANK. You're a mysterious kid. Where did you learn the fighting game?

JOE. These past two years, all over the city—in the gyms ——

BONAPARTE. Hey, Joe, you sounda like crazy! You no gotta nature for fight. You're musician. Whata you say, heh? Whata you do?

JOE. Let's call it a day.

BONAPARTE. Isa no true whata I say ——?

JOE. That's all for tonight. (*His lips tightened, he abruptly exits.*)

BONAPARTE. (*Calling after him.*) Take a gooda sleep, Joe.

FRANK. (*Smiling.*) It looks like the gold bug has visited our house.

CARP. (*Sadly.*) Fortunes! I used to hear it in my youth—the streets of America are paved with gold. Say, you forgot to give him the present.

BONAPARTE. (*Slowly, puzzled.*) I don'ta know . . . he say he gonna fight. . . .

SLOW FADEOUT

ACT I

SCENE 3

Two months later, MOODY'S *office as in Act 1, Scene 1.*[1] MOODY *is pacing back and forth in one of his fuming moods. Those present include* LORNA, *stretched out on*

[1] See Production Notes, p. 4.

the couch, blowing cigarette smoke into the air, TOKIO *sitting quietly on a chair, and* ROXY GOTTLIEB, *comfortably spread out in the desk chair, wearing a big white panama hat which he seldom removes.*

ROXY. They don't like him. They seen him in five fights already. He's a clever boy, that Bonaparte, and speedy—but he's first-class lousy in the shipping department! I bought a piece of him, so I got a right to say it: a mosquito gives out better! Did you read what he wrote in his column, that Drake? He writes he's a regular " brain trust."

LORNA. What's wrong with that?

ROXY. I'll tell you in a capsule: the people who'll pay to watch a " brain trust " you could fit in a telephone booth! Roxy Gottlieb is telling you!

MOODY. Roxy's right. Joe pulls his punches. Two months already and he don't throw his hands right and he don't throw them enough.

LORNA. Tom, what do you want the boy to do? You surely know by now he's not a slugger. His main asset is his science—he's a student.

ROXY. (*Loftily.*) Excuse me, Miss Moon. In the prizefight ring the cash customer don't look for stoodents. Einstein lives in a college—a wonderful man in *his* line! Also, while I think of it, a woman's place is in the hay, not in the office!

MOODY. (*Indignantly.*) Where do you come off to make a remark like that?

LORNA. (*Standing up.*) At the moment a woman's place is in the bar—see you later. (*She looks at others with a peculiar smile and exits.* MOODY *stares at* ROXY *who realizes he has said the wrong thing.*)

MOODY. I'm worried about that boy!

TOKIO. I'd trust him, Tom. Joe knows his own needs, as he says. Don't ask him to change his style. A style is best when it's individual, when it comes out of the inner personality and the lay of the muscles and the set of the bones. That boy stands a chance to make the best lightweight since Benny Simon.

ROXY. On *your* nose!

TOKIO. He's got one of the best defenses I ever seen. And speedy as the wind.

MOODY. But he won't fight!

ROXY. A momma doll gives out better!

TOKIO. He's a peculiar duck—I want him thinking he's the best thing in shoe leather.

MOODY. He thinks so now.

TOKIO. I don't like to contradict you, Tom, but he don't. It's seventy-five percent front. If you want the goods delivered you have to treat him delicate, gentle—like a girl.

ROXY. Like a girl? Why didn't you say so before?

MOODY. No, Roxy, not you—you just treat him like a human being.

TOKIO. I think we can begin the build-up now.

MOODY. A road tour?

TOKIO. I'd like to take him around the Middle West, about fifteen bouts.

ROXY. (*Answering a look from* MOODY.) I didn't say no. But will he cooperate?

TOKIO. As soon as I find the password.

MOODY. What's the password to make this kid go in and slug— that's the problem. (*There is a knock at the door.* MOODY *calls.*) Yes? (*Door opens and* BONAPARTE *stands there hesitantly.*)

BONAPARTE. (*Timidly.*) My name is Joe Bonaparte's father. I come-a to see my son's new friends.

MOODY. (*Expansively.*) Come in, sit down, Mr. Bonaparte.

ROXY. (*Sitting comfortably.*) Take a seat.

BONAPARTE. Am I interrupt?

MOODY. Not at all.

ROXY. What's the matter with your boy?

TOKIO. (*To* BONAPARTE.) This is Mr. Moody and Mr. Gottlieb.

BONAPARTE. (*Sitting.*) Good afternoon.

MOODY. We were just discussing your son.

BONAPARTE. I please to hear. I like find out froma you how's this boxer business for Joe. Whata good in it for him.

MOODY. Your Joe's a very clever fighter.

ROXY. Can you take it? We want to make your boy famous—a millionaire, but he won't let us—won't cooperate. How do you like it?

BONAPARTE. Why? Whatta he do?

ROXY. (*Going over and facing the old man in a lecturing position.*) I'll ask *you*. What does he do? What does he do that's right? *Nothing!* We offer him on a gold platter! Wine, women and song, to make a figure of speech. We offer him *magnitudes!* . . .

BONAPARTE. (*Waiting.*) Yes ——?

MOODY. But he won't fight.

BONAPARTE. (*Puzzled.*) He'sa fighta for you, no?

ROXY. You're right—no! Your boy's got unexplored possibilities—*unexplored!* But you can't make a purse out of somebody's ear.

MOODY. (*Trying to counteract* ROXY'S *volubility.*) My colleague is trying to say that Joe keeps holding back in the ring.

BONAPARTE. Holda back?

TOKIO. He nurses his self ——

MOODY. He keeps holding back ——

TOKIO. His defense is brilliant ——

MOODY. Gorgeous ——!

ROXY. But where's the offense? You take but you can't give. Figure it out—where would you be in a traffic jam? You know how to reverse—but to shift in second or high?—nothing!

BONAPARTE. (*Quietly to* ROXY.) Hey, you talka too much—nobody's contradicta you.

ROXY. (*After a momentary setback.*) "Everybody'sa contradicta me!" Even you, and I never met you before. (*With a reproachful glance he retires to desk where he sits and sulks.*)

BONAPARTE. (*Singling out* TOKIO *as a man to whom he can speak.*) Who are you?

TOKIO. Your son's trainer. . . .

BONAPARTE. You interest to helpa my boy?

TOKIO. (*Respectfully.*) Very much. . . .

BONAPARTE. Me too. Maybe not so as plan by these-a gentleman here. I don't say price fight'sa no good for Joe. Joe like-a to be fame, not feel ashame. . . .

TOKIO. Is Joe afraid of his hands?

BONAPARTE. I don't know. You tella me what'sa what . . . I don't know price fight. His hand coulda get hurt?

MOODY. Every fighter hurts his hands. Sometimes they break ——

TOKIO. They heal up in no time.

ROXY. (*Flaring out.*) What's so special about hands? I suppose your kid plays piano!

BONAPARTE. Coulda get hurt? Coulda break?!

ROXY. So what?

BONAPARTE. (*Up on his feet.*) Hey, you! I don't like-a you! You

22

no interest in my boy! (*Proudly.*) My boy'sa besta violin' in New York!

MOODY. (*Suddenly sickened.*) What . . . ?

BONAPARTE. Yes, play the violin!

MOODY. That's it! . . .

ROXY. (*Anguished by this stupidity.*) If I had hair I'd tear it out! Five hundred fiddlers stand on Broadway and 48th Street, on the corner, every day, rain or shine, hot or cold. And your boy dares ——! (*Turning to* MOODY.) How do you like it? (*He waves his hands in despair and retires to desk, where he sits in fuming disgusted silence.*)

MOODY. (*Repressing a feeling of triumph.*) Your boy's afraid of his hands because he fiddles?

BONAPARTE. Yes, musta be!

TOKIO. Why did you come and tell us this?

BONAPARTE. Because I like-a to help my boy. I like-a for him to try himself out. Maybe thisa better business for him. Maybe not. He mus' try to find out, to see whata he want . . . I don't know. Don't help Joe to tell him I come here. Don't say it. (*He slowly walks to door.*)

MOODY. That means you won't stand in his way?

BONAPARTE. My boy coulda break his hand? Gentleman, I'ma not so happy as you . . . no! (*He slowly exits.*)

MOODY. (*Joyously.*) I'm beginning to see the light! Joe's mind ain't made up that the fist is mightier than the fiddle.

ROXY. (*Bouncing up and down.*) I'll make up his mind. For the money that's involved I'd make Niagara Falls turn around and go back to Canada.

TOKIO. Don't try to bully him into anything.

ROXY. In Roxy Gottlieb he met his match.

MOODY. (*Explosively.*) What the hell's the matter with you, Roxy! Sit down a minute. (ROXY *sits.*) As I see it, the job is to handle him gently, to make him see how much we prize him—to kill his doubts with goodness.

ROXY. I got it: the password is honey! . . .

MOODY. Right! The Middle West tour is on! Tokio goes along to build up a real offensive. I take care of the newspapers here. Chris', I thought it was something serious! I'm getting to feel like 1928 again. Call it intuition: I feel like the Resurrection. (*He gets up and begins to stroll about.*) Once we're out of the tunnel, with thirty bouts behind us ——

ROXY. If you hear a noise, it's my mouth watering —— (*The telephone rings.* MOODY *answers.*)

MOODY. Hello? . . . Yeah . . . I think he'll win —— (*Hangs up.*) Who do you think that was? (*Imitating.*) "Fuseli is speaking." Eddie Fuseli!

ROXY. Fuseli? What's he want?

MOODY. Will Joe win against Vincenti Tuesday. Tokio, from now on it's your job.

TOKIO. I got faith in the boy.

MOODY. (*To* ROXY.) I have to ask one thing—when Joe comes over from the gym let me do the talking.

TOKIO. And don't mention music! (LORNA *enters.*)

LORNA. Shh! Here's Joe. (JOE BONAPARTE *enters the office. Immediately* MOODY *and* ROXY *put on their softest kid gloves. Their methods of salesmanship will shortly become so apparent that both* JOE *and* LORNA *become suspicious.*)

MOODY. (*Slowly circling around.*) Glad to see you, Joe. Joe, you remember in reference to what we were speaking about yesterday? Well . . . we had several friends on the long distance phone. We're booking fifteen out of town bouts for you. Tough ones, too.

ROXY. Tonight I'm calling my Chicago connections.

MOODY. We talked it over with Tokio and he says—well, tell him what you said, Tokio—tell him the truth.

TOKIO. I think you got a wonderful future.

MOODY. (*To* TOKIO.) Name the names, Tokio.

TOKIO. Well, I said Benny Simon—as good as Simon, I said.

MOODY. Tokio's gonna work with you—help you develop a right ——

ROXY. And a left! What'sa right without a left?

MOODY. Tokio thinks that when he brings you back you'll be a contender for Number One.

JOE. (*A little defensively.*) Really? . . .

MOODY. But *you* have to help *us* help *you.*

ROXY. Could Webster say it better?

MOODY. (*Softly singing a siren song, his arms around* JOE's *shoulders.*) This job needs gorgeous concentration. All your time and thoughts, Joe. No side lines, no side interests ——

24

JOE. (*Defensively.*) I don't go out with girls.

MOODY. You're in the fighting game. It's like being a priest—your work comes first. What would you rather do than fight?

JOE. (*Defensively.*) I don't know what you mean.

MOODY. (*Carefully picking his words.*) Some boys, for instance, like to save their looks. They'd practically throw the fight to keep their nose intact.

JOE. (*Smiling wryly.*) My looks don't interest me. (LORNA *is listening with rapt attention.*)

MOODY. (*Still singing the siren song.*) Then what's holding you back, Joe? You can tell me, Joe. We've set up housekeeping together, Joe, and I want you to tell me if you can't cook a steak—it don't matter. We're married anyway. . . .

JOE. (*Uneasily.*) Who's being put to bed?

MOODY. What do you mean?

JOE. I don't like this seduction scene. (*To* TOKIO.) What are they after?

TOKIO. They think you're afraid of your hands.

MOODY. Are you?

JOE. Half . . .

TOKIO. Why?

ROXY. (*Bouncing up.*) Tell the truth!

JOE. What truth?

MOODY. (*Holding back* ROXY *with a look.*) Are you afraid your hands'll bust, Joe? (JOE *remains silent.*) What's a busted hand to a fighter? You can't go in and do your best if you're scared of your mitts . . . can you? You tell me. . . .

JOE. No. . . .

MOODY. Whyn't you give up outside ideas, Joe?

ROXY. (*Suddenly, in a loud voice to* TOKIO.) You shoulda seen that bunch of musicians on 48th Street before. Fiddlers, drummers, cornetists—not a dime in a car-load. Bums in the park! Oh, excuse me, Tom, I was just telling Tokio —— (JOE *is now aware that the others know of the violin. Now he is completely closed to them.* MOODY *sees this. He says to* ROXY:)

MOODY. (*Wrathfully.*) What would you like to say, my fine-feathered friend?

ROXY. (*Simulating bewilderment.*) What's the matter? What happened? (*Receiving no answer, he looks around several times and adds, with a shrug:*) I think I'll run across the street and pick up an eight-cylinder lunch.

MOODY. Sprinkle it with arsenic. Do that for me, for me, sweetheart!!

ROXY. (*Hurt.*) That's a fine remark from a friend. (*He haughtily exits.*)

JOE. What do you want, Mr. Moody?

MOODY. At the moment, nothing. I'm puffed out. See you tomorrow over the gym.

JOE. Maybe I won't be there. I might give up fighting as a bad job. I'm not over-convinced it's what I want. I can do other things. . . .

TOKIO. I'll see you tomorrow at the gym, Joe. (JOE *looks at both the men, says nothing, exits.*) That Mr. Gottlieb is a case. See you later.

MOODY. (*Not looking up.*) Okay. (TOKIO *exits.* LORNA *and* MOODY *are alone. She blows cigarette smoke to the ceiling.* MOODY *puts his feet up on desk and leans back wearily. Snorting through his nostrils.*) The password is honey!

LORNA. What was that all about? (*Telephone rings.*)

MOODY. (*Of the ringing bell.*) If that's for me, tear it up. I ain't in, not even for God.

LORNA. (*Answering.*) Hello? . . . (*Putting her hand on mouthpiece.*) It's Mrs. God—your wife. (MOODY *makes a grimace of distaste but picks up phone and puts on a sweet voice.*)

MOODY. Yes, Monica darling. . . . Yeah . . . you and your support. . . . You're gonna fifty-buck me to death! . . . Monica, if I had fifty bucks I'd buy myself a big juicy coffin.—What?—So throw me in jail. (*He bangs up phone.*) Bitch! That'll be time number three. She means it too.

LORNA. What was that scene with Bonaparte?

MOODY. Sweetheart, the jig is up! Believe it or not, Bonaparte's a violinist. Maybe he was on the radio. I don't know what the hell he was. His old man came here and told us. His mitts are on his mind. You can't do a thing with a nut like that.

LORNA. Won't he give up the violin?

MOODY. You heard him stalling. This is the end, Lorna. It's our last chance for a decent life, for getting married—we have to make that kid fight! He's more than a meal ticket—he's every-

26

thing we want and need from life! (LORNA *goes over and slaps him on the back.*)

LORNA. Put up your chin, little man.

MOODY. Don't Brisbane me, Lorna. I'm licked. I'm tired. Find me a mouse hole to crawl in. . . .

LORNA. Why don't you ask me when you want something? You got the brains of a flea. Do you want Bonaparte to fight?

MOODY. Do I wanna see tomorrow?

LORNA. I'll make him fight.

MOODY. How?

LORNA. How? . . . I'm "a tramp from Newark," Tom. . . . I know a dozen ways. . . .

SLOW FADEOUT

ACT I

SCENE 4

A few nights later.

JOE *and* LORNA *sit on a bench in the park.*[1] *It is night. There is carousel music*[2] *in the distance. Cars*[3] *ride by the boy and girl in the late spring night. Out of sight a traffic light changes from red to green and back again throughout the scene and casts its colors on the faces of the boy and girl.*

LORNA. Success and fame! Or just a lousy living. You're lucky you won't have to worry about those things. . . .

JOE. Won't I?

LORNA. Unless Tom Moody's a liar.

JOE. You like him, don't you?

LORNA. (*After a pause.*) I like him.

JOE. I like how you dress. The girls look nice in the summer time. Did you ever stand at the Fifth Avenue Library and watch those girls go by?

LORNA. No, I never did. (*Switching the subject.*) That's the

[1] See Production Notes, p. 4.

[2], [3] See copyright page for record data.

27

carousel, that music. Did you ever ride on one of those?

JOE. That's for kids.

LORNA. Weren't you ever a kid, for God's sake?

JOE. Not a happy kid.

LORNA. Why?

JOE. Well, I always felt different. Even my name was special—Bonaparte—and my eyes . . .

LORNA. I wouldn't have taken that too serious. . . . (*There is a silent pause.* JOE *looks straight ahead.*)

JOE. Gee, all those cars . . .

LORNA. Lots of horses trot around here. The rich know how to live. You'll be rich. . . .

JOE. My brother Frank is an organizer for the C.I.O.

LORNA. What's that?

JOE. If you worked in a factory you'd know. Did you ever work?

LORNA. (*With a smile.*) No, when I came out of the cocoon I was a butterfly and butterflies don't work.

JOE. All those cars . . . whizz, whizz. (*Now turning less casual.*) Where's Mr. Moody tonight?

LORNA. He goes up to see his kid on Tuesday nights. It's a sick kid, a girl. His wife leaves it at her mother's house.

JOE. That leaves you free, don't it?

LORNA. What are you hinting at?

JOE. I'm thinking about you and Mr. Moody.

LORNA. Why think about it? I don't. Why should you?

JOE. If you belonged to me I wouldn't think about it.

LORNA. Haven't you got a girl?

JOE. No.

LORNA. Why not?

JOE. (*Evasively.*) Oh . . .

LORNA. Tokio says you're going far in the fighting game.

JOE. Music means more to me. May I tell you something?

LORNA. Of course.

JOE. If you laugh I'll never speak to you again.

LORNA. I'm not the laughing type.

JOE. With music I'm never alone when I'm alone —— Playing music . . . that's like saying, "I am man. I belong here. How do you do, World—good evening!" When I play music nothing is closed to me. I'm not afraid of people and what they say.

There's no war in music. It's not like the streets. Does this sound funny?

LORNA. No.

JOE. But when you leave your room . . . down in the street . . . it's war! Music can't help me there. Understand?

LORNA. Yes.

JOE. People have hurt my feelings for years. I never forget. You can't get even with people by playing the fiddle. If music shot bullets I'd like it better—artists and people like that are freaks today. The world moves fast and they sit around like forgotten dopes.

LORNA. You're loaded with fireworks. Why don't you fight?

JOE. You have to be what you are ——!

LORNA. Fight! See what happens ——

JOE. Or end up in the bughouse!

LORNA. God's teeth! Who says you have to be one thing?

JOE. My nature isn't fighting!

LORNA. Don't Tokio know what he's talking about? Don't Tom? Joe, listen: be a fighter! Show the world! If you made your fame and fortune—and you can—you'd be anything you want. Do it! Bang your way to the lightweight crown. Get a bank account. Hire a great doctor with a beard—get your eyes fixed ——

JOE. What's the matter with my eyes?

LORNA. Excuse me, I stand corrected. (*After a pause.*) You get mad all the time.

JOE. That's from thinking about myself.

LORNA. How old are you, Joe?

JOE. Twenty-one and a half, and the months are going fast.

LORNA. You're very smart for twenty-one and a half " and the months are going fast."

JOE. Why not? I read every page of the Encyclopaedia Britannica. My father's friend, Mr. Carp, has it. A shrimp with glasses had to do something.

LORNA. I'd like to meet your father. Your mother dead?

JOE. Yes.

LORNA. So is mine.

JOE. Where do you come from? The city is full of girls who look as if they never had parents.

LORNA. I'm a girl from over the river. My father is still alive—

29

shucking oysters and bumming drinks somewhere in the wilds of Jersey. I'll tell you a secret: I don't like you.

JOE. (Surprised.) Why?

LORNA. You're too sufficient by yourself . . . too inside yourself.

JOE. You like it or you don't.

LORNA. You're on an island ——

JOE. Robinson Crusoe . . .

LORNA. That's right—" me, myself, and I." Why not come out and see the world?

JOE. Does it seem that way?

LORNA. Can't you see yourself?

JOE. No. . . .

LORNA. Take a bird's-eye view; you don't know what's right or wrong. You don't know what to pick, but you won't admit it.

JOE. Do you?

LORNA. Leave me out. This is the anatomy of Joe Bonaparte.

JOE. You're dancing on my nose, huh?

LORNA. Shall I stop?

JOE. No.

LORNA. You're a miserable creature. You want your arm in gelt up to the elbow. You'll take fame so people won't laugh or scorn your face. You'd give your soul for those things. But every time you turn your back your little soul kicks you in the teeth. It don't give in so easy.

JOE. And what does your soul do in its perfumed vanity case?

LORNA. Forget about me.

JOE. Don't you want ——?

LORNA. (Suddenly nasty.) I told you forget it!

JOE. (Quietly.) Moody sent you after me—a decoy! You made a mistake, Lorna, for two reasons. I made up my own mind to fight. Point two, he doesn't know you don't love him ——

LORNA. You're a fresh kid.

JOE. In fact he doesn't know anything about you at all.

LORNA. (Challengingly.) But you do?

JOE. This is the anatomy of Lorna Moon: she's a lost baby. She doesn't know what's right or wrong. She's a miserable creature who never knew what to pick. But she'd never admit it. And I'll tell you why you picked Moody!

LORNA. You don't know what you're talking about.

JOE. Go home, Lorna. If you stay, I'll know something about you. . . .

LORNA. You don't know anything.

JOE. Now's your chance—go home!

LORNA. Tom loves me.

JOE. (*After a long silence, looking ahead.*) I'm going to buy a car.

LORNA. They make wonderful cars today. Even the lizzies ——

JOE. Gary Cooper's got the kind I want. I saw it in the paper, but it costs too much—fourteen thousand. If I found one second-hand ——

LORNA. And if you had the cash ——

JOE. I'll get it ——

LORNA. Sure, if you'd go in and really fight!

JOE. (*In a sudden burst.*) Tell your Mr. Moody I'll dazzle the eyes out of his head!

LORNA. You mean it?

JOE. (*Looking out ahead.*) Those cars are poison in my blood. When you sit in a car and speed you're looking down at the world. Speed, speed, everything is speed—nobody gets me!

LORNA. You mean in the ring?

JOE. In or out, nobody gets me! Gee, I like to stroke that gas!

LORNA. You sound like Jack the Ripper.

JOE. (*Standing up suddenly.*) I'll walk you back to your house—your hotel, I mean. (LORNA *stands.* JOE *continues.*) Do you have the same room?

LORNA. (*With sneaking admiration.*) You're a fresh kid!

JOE. When you're lying in his arms tonight, tell him, for me, that the next World's Champ is feeding in his stable.

LORNA. Did you really read those Brittannia books?

JOE. From A to Z.

LORNA. And you're only twenty-one?

JOE. And a half.

LORNA. Something's wrong somewhere.

JOE. I know. . . . (*They slowly walk out as*)

FADEOUT

ACT I

SCENE 5

The next week.
It is near midnight in the dining room of the Bonaparte
home. Same as Act I, Scene 2. An open suitcase rests
on table. SIGGIE *is pouring samples of wine for* LORNA
MOON. *He himself drinks appreciatively. To one side sits*
BONAPARTE *silently, thoughtfully, watchfully—pretend-*
ing to read the newspaper.

SIGGIE. I was fit to be knocked down with a feather when I heard
it. I couldn't believe it until I seen him fight over at the Keystone
last week. You never know what somebody's got in him—like the
man with germs—suddenly he's down in bed with a crisis! (JOE
enters with an armful of clothes which he begins to pack in suit-
case.)
LORNA. Joe's road tour will do him lots of good. (ANNA *enters and*
takes off an apron. Silence, in which SIGGIE *and* LORNA *sip their*
wine.)
ANNA. How do you like that wine, Miss Moon? My father makes
better wine than any Eyetalian in New York. My father knows
everything—don't you, poppa? (*With a faint smile,* BONAPARTE
shrugs his shoulders.)
SIGGIE. We're thinking of sending the old man to a leper
colony. . . .
ANNA. Don't my husband say funny things? Tell her what you
told the janitor Tuesday, Siggie.
SIGGIE. Never mind, never mind.
ANNA. You know how I met Siggie? He was a United Cigar Store
clerk and I walked in for a pack of Camels and the first thing
you know he said something funny. It was raw, so I can't say it.
He had me laughing from the first. Seven years and I haven't
stopped laughing yet. (*She laughs loudly, pleasurably.*) This will
be the first time Joe ever went traveling. Was you ever out of
New York, Miss Moon?
LORNA. Oh, many times.
ANNA. That's nice. Far?

LORNA. California, Detroit, Chicago. I was an airplane hostess for two months.

ANNA. That's nice—it's a real adventure. I'd like to fly.

SIGGIE. Stay on the ground! Fly! What for? Who do you know up there? Eagles?

ANNA. It must be a wonderful way to see life.

LORNA. (*Drinking.*) I've seen life in all its aspects. (BONAPARTE *stands up with a smile.* LORNA'S *eyes follow him as he exits. To* JOE.) I think your father left because he don't like me.

JOE. He likes you.

ANNA. My father likes everybody. He's a very deep man. My father has more friends than any man alive. But best of all he likes his horse, Dolly, who drives the fruit wagon. My father can't sit still on Sunday afternoon—he has to go see what that horse is doing. (*Her eyes catch sight of suitcase.*) Joe, you don't know how to pack. (*She starts over to assist him.*)

SIGGIE. (*Querulously.*) Rest the feet awhile, Duchess.

ANNA. (*Explaining her move.*) He don't know how to pack. (*Beginning to rearrange suitcase.* BONAPARTE *returns and hands* JOE *a sweater.*)

BONAPARTE. You forget your good sweater.

JOE. Thanks. (BONAPARTE *sits.* JOE *looks at him sideways.*)

ANNA. When you get out to Chicago, buy yourself some new underwear, Joe. I hear everything's cheaper in Chicago. Is that right, Miss Moon?

LORNA. (*After taking another drink.*) Chicago? I don't know. I was there only one night—I got news that night my mother died As a matter of fact, she killed herself.

ANNA. That's very sad.

LORNA. No, my father's an old drunk son-of-a-bitch. Did you ask me about my father?

BONAPARTE. (*Who has been listening intently.*) Yes. . . .

LORNA. Twice a week he kicked my mother's face in. If I let myself go I'd be a drunkard in a year.

ANNA. My father never said one bad word to my mother in her whole lifetime. And she was a big nuisance right up till the day she died. She was more like me, more on the stout 'side. Take care of your health, Joe, when you're out there. What's better than health?

33

LORNA. (*Turning to* BONAPARTE, *with whom she is self-conscious.*) The question is, do you like me or do you not?

BONAPARTE. (*With a faint smile.*) Yes. . . .

LORNA. Your family is very cute —— Now do you like me?

BONAPARTE. Yes. . . .

LORNA. Why do you look at me that way?

BONAPARTE. I don't look special. You gonna travel on those train with my son?

LORNA. God's teeth, no! I'm a friend of his manager's, that's all. And a friend of Joe's too.

BONAPARTE. You are in favor for my son to prizefight? (JOE *looks at his father sideways and exits.*)

LORNA. Certainly. Aren't you?

BONAPARTE. Joe has a dream many year to be superior violin'. Was it boyhood thing? Was it real? Or is this real now? Those are-a my question, Miss Moon. Maybe you are friend to my son. Then I aska you, look out for him. Study him. Help him find what'sa right. Tell me, Miss Moon, when you find out. Help Joe find truthful success. Will you do it for me?

LORNA. I'll be glad to keep my eye on him. (JOE *enters with slippers, which he puts in bag.*)

ANNA. (*To* JOE.) You could stand some new shirts, too.

SIGGIE. Listen, pop, I'm a natural man and I don't like wise guys. Joe went in the boxing game 'cause he's ashamed to be poor. That's his way to enter a little enterprise. All other remarks are so much alfalfa! (JOE *locks bag.*)

ANNA. (*Taking wine glass from* SIGGIE's *hand.*) Drunk as a horse fly!

JOE. It's getting late and the train won't wait.

SIGGIE. (*Standing up.*) My God is success. Need I say more? I'm prouda you, Joe. Come home a champ. Make enough dough to buy your sister's boy friend a new cab. Yes, boys and girls, I'm looking in that old crystal ball and I see strange and wonderful events! Yazoo!

ANNA. (*Giggling.*) Drunk as a horse fly!

JOE. (*To* SIGGIE.) You can't drive us down to the station in this condition.

SIGGIE. What condition?

ANNA. You're drunk, stupid.

SIGGIE. Shut the face, foolish! Just because I don't hold in my

34

nerves she thinks I'm drunk. If you hold in your nerves you get ulcers. (*To* JOE.) Get your "chapow" and let's go. Or don't you want me to drive you down?

JOE. No.

SIGGIE. I should worry—my cab's in the garage anyway! (*Suddenly he sits.*)

JOE. We'd better start. . . .

LORNA. (*To* BONAPARTE.) I'd like to have another talk with you sometime.

BONAPARTE. Come any time in the evening. You are a very lovely girl. (MR. CARP *stands in the doorway.*) Here is Mr. Carp to say good-bye.

SIGGIE. Come in, my little prince.

CARP. (*Coming in and shaking hands with* JOE.) I wish you good luck in every undertaking.

JOE. (*Uneasily, because his father is looking at him.*) Thanks.

BONAPARTE. (*Introducing* CARP.) Miss Moon, my neighbor, Mr. Carp.

CARP. A pleasure to meet you.

LORNA. Hello. (BONAPARTE *brings violin case from its hiding place in buffet.*)

BONAPARTE. Joe, I buy you this some time ago. Don't give cause I don't know whatta you gonna do. Take him with you now. Play for yourself. It gonna remember you your old days of musical life. (JOE *puts down suitcase and picks up violin. He plucks the strings, he tightens one of them. In spite of the tension his face turns soft and tender.*)

LORNA. (*Watching intently.*) We better not miss the train—Tokio's waiting.

BONAPARTE. (*Of violin.*) Take him with you, Joe.

JOE. It's beautiful. . . .

BONAPARTE. Practice on the road. (JOE *abruptly turns and with the violin exits. The others listen, each standing in his place, as rich violin music [1] comes from the other room.* JOE *returns. There is silence as he places the violin on the table in front of his father.*)

JOE. (*In a low voice.*) Return it, poppa.

ANNA. (*Hugging* JOE.) Have a good trip, Joey.

CARP. Eat in good restaurants. . . . (*There is silence: the father*

---

[1] Any good *solo* violin music may be used here.

35

and son look at each other. The others in the room sense the drama between the two. Finally:)

JOE. I have to do this, poppa.

BONAPARTE. (*To* JOE.) Be careful fora your hands.

JOE. Poppa, give me the word ——

BONAPARTE. What word?

JOE. Give me the word to go ahead. You're looking at yesterday—I see tomorrow. Maybe you think I ought to spend my whole life here—you and Carp blowing off steam.

BONAPARTE. (*Holding himself back.*) Oh, Joe, shut your mouth!

JOE. Give me the word to go ahead!

BONAPARTE. Be careful fora your hands!

JOE. I want you to give me the word!

BONAPARTE. (*Crying out.*) No! No word! You gonna fight? All right! Okay! But I don't gonna give no word! No!

JOE. That's how you feel?

BONAPARTE. That'sa how I feel! (BONAPARTE'S *voice breaks and there is nothing for father and son to do but to clutch each other in a hasty embrace. Finally* BONAPARTE *disentangles himself and turns away.* JOE *abruptly grabs up his suitcase and exits.* LORNA *follows, stopping at the door to look back at* BONAPARTE. *In the ensuing silence* ANNA *looks at her father and shakes her head.* SIGGIE *suddenly lumbers to his feet and sounds off like a chime.*)

SIGGIE. Gong gong gong gong!

ANNA. Gee, poppa . . .

SIGGIE. Come to bed, Anna. . . . Anna-banana . . . (SIGGIE *exits.*)

ANNA. Gee, poppa . . . (*She touches her father sympathetically.*)

BONAPARTE. (*Without turning.*) Gone to bed, Anna. . . . (ANNA *slowly exits.* BONAPARTE *now slowly comes back to the table and looks down at violin.*)

CARP. (*Seating himself slowly.*) Come, my friend . . . we will have a nice talk on a cultural topic. (*Looking at the violin.*) You'll work around a number of years before you make it up, the price of that fiddle. (BONAPARTE *stands looking down at violin. Sadly.*) Yes, my friend, what is man? As Schopenhauer says, and in the last analysis . . .

SLOW FADEOUT

ACT II

SCENE 1

Six months later. Present in the corner of a gymnasium [1] are ROXY, MOODY, LORNA *and* TOKIO. *They are looking off right, watching* JOE BONAPARTE *work out with a partner. From off right come the sounds of typical gym activities: the thud of boxing gloves, the rat-a-tat of the punching bag, and from time to time the general bell [2] which is a signal for rest periods. Tacked on the tin walls are an ad for Everlast boxing equipment, boxing " card " placards, a soiled American flag, some faded exit signs.*

The group watches silently for several seconds after the lights fade in. A BOXER, *wiping his perspiring body with a towel, passes from left to right and looks back at* LORNA'S *legs. As* ROXY *watches, his head moves to and fro in the rhythm of* JOE'S *sparring off stage* R. ROXY *nods his head in admiration.*

ROXY. Tokio. I gotta give the devil his dues: in the past six months you done a noble job!

TOKIO. (*Calling off.*) With the left! A long left, Joe! . . .

LORNA. (*Looking off.*) Joe's a very good-looking boy. I never quite noticed it before. (*General bell sounds, the boxing din off stage stops.*)

MOODY. (*Rubbing his hands enthusiastically.*) " Let it rain, let it pour! It ain't gonna rain where we're headed for! "

ROXY. I'm tickled to death to see the canary birds left his gloves.

TOKIO. He's the king of all he surveys.

MOODY. Boy, oh, boy, how he surprised them in the Bronx last

¹ See Production Notes, p. 4.
² See copyright page for sound effect records.

night! . . . But one thing I can't explain—that knockout he took in Philly five weeks ago.

TOKIO. That night he was off his feed, Tom. Where do you see speed like that? That's style, real style—you can't tag him. And he's giving it with both hands.

MOODY. You don't have to sell me his virtues—I'm sold. Nevertheless, he got tagged in Philly.

TOKIO. Here's what happened there: we run into some man when we're leaving the hotel. Joe goes pale. I ask him what it is. "Nothing," he says. But I see for myself—a man with long hair and a violin case. When we turn the corner, he says, "He's after me," he says. As if it's cops and robbers! (*The general bell sounds, the fighting din begins again.*)

ROXY. A kidnapper?

LORNA. Don't be a fool. He was reminded . . .

ROXY. Speak when spoken to, Miss Moon!

MOODY. (*Moodily.*) And when he got in the ring that night, he kept his hands in his pockets?

TOKIO. Yeah. I didn't mention this before—it's not important.

MOODY. But it's still a danger ——

TOKIO. No. No.

MOODY. But anyway, we better get him away from his home. We can't afford no more possible bad showings at this stage of the game. No more apparitions, like suddenly a fiddle flies across the room on wings! (*The group again intently watches* JOE *off stage.*) Ooh! Did you see that? He's packing a real Sunday punch in that right. (*Calling off.*) Hit 'im, Joe, hit 'im! (*As an indistinct answer comes back.*) Ha ha, looka that, hahaha . . . (*Now turning to* TOKIO.) What's your idea of a match with Lombardo?

TOKIO. Can you get it?

MOODY. Maybe.

TOKIO. Get it.

MOODY. Sure?

TOKIO. It's an easy win, on points at least. (*During the last few lines a thin dark man has entered. His dark hair is grayed at the temples, an inarticulate look in his face. He is* EDDIE FUSELI, *a renowned gambler and gunman.*)

EDDIE FUSELI. (*Approaching the group.*) Hello.

ROXY. (*Nervously.*) Hello, Eddie.

MOODY. (*Turning.*) I haven't seen you for a dog's age, Fuseli.

EDDIE. (*Pointing off stage.*) You got this certain boy—Bonaparte. I like his looks. American born?

ROXY. Right from here.

EDDIE. (*Watching* JOE *off.*) Like a cat, never off his position. He appeals to me. (*To* MOODY.) They call you the Brown Fox. What's your opinion of this boy?

MOODY. (*Coolly, on guard.*) Possibilities . . .

EDDIE. (*To* TOKIO.) What's your idea?

TOKIO. Tom said it.

EDDIE. Could he get on top?

MOODY. (*As above.*) I can't see that far ahead. I don't read palms.

EDDIE. Could I buy a piece?

MOODY. No.

EDDIE. (*Coolly.*) Could I?

MOODY. No!

EDDIE. (*With a certain tenderness.*) I like a good fighter. I like to see you after, Tom. (*Of* LORNA.) This your girl?

LORNA. (*Pertly.*) I'm my mother's girl.

EDDIE. (*With a small mirthless laugh.*) Ha ha—that's a hot one. (*He coolly drifts out of the scene on his cat's feet. General bell sounds. The din ceases.*)

LORNA. What exhaust pipe did he crawl out of?

ROXY. I remember this Eddie Fuseli when he came back from the war with a gun. He's still got the gun and he still gives me goose pimples!

MOODY. That Fuseli's a black mark in my book. Every once in a while he shoots across my quiet existence like a roman candle!

LORNA. Sell or don't sell. But better be careful, that guy's tough! (*A* FIGHTER, *robed, hooded with towel, passes across: A* GAMBLING TYPE *passes in the opposite direction. Both look at* LORNA'S *legs.*)

MOODY. Give a rat like that a finger and you lose a hand before you know it!

TOKIO. Did you know Joe bought a car this morning?

ROXY. What kinda car?

TOKIO. A Deusenberg.

MOODY. One of those fancy speed wagons?

TOKIO. (*Agreeing.*) It cost him five grand, second-hand.

MOODY. (*Flaring up.*) Am I a step-child around here? I'm glad you tell me now, if only outa courtesy!

ROXY. (*Indignantly.*) Whatta you keep a thing like that incognito for?

MOODY. He drives like a maniac! That time we drove to Long Beach? I almost lost my scalp! We can't let him drive around like that! Boy, he's getting a bushel of bad habits! We gotta be careful. (*The general bell sounds again, the fighting din stops.*) Here's the truth: our boy can be the champ in three easy lessons—Lombardo, Fulton, the Chocolate Drop. But we gotta be careful!

LORNA. Here he comes. (JOE *enters in bathrobe, taking off his headgear, which* TOKIO *takes from him.*)

MOODY. (*Completely changing his tone.*) You looked very good in there, Joe. You're going swell and I like it. I'd work more with that long left if I were you.

JOE. Yes, I was speaking to Tokio about that. I feel my form's improving. I like to work. I'm getting somewhere—I feel it better every day.

LORNA. Happy?

JOE. (*Looking at her intently.*) Every day's Saturday!

ROXY. (*Officiously.*) Say, what's this I hear you bought a Deusenberg?

JOE. What's your objection—I might have some fun?

ROXY. I got my wampum on you. I like to know your habits. Ain't I permitted? (JOE *is about to retort hotly when* MOODY *gently takes his arm in an attempt to soothe him.*)

MOODY. Wait a minute, Joe. After all we have your welfare at heart. And after all a Deusenberg can go one fifty per —— (EDDIE FUSELI *appears above, unseen by the others. He listens.*)

JOE. Who'd want to drive that fast?

MOODY. And since we're vitally interested in your future ——

JOE. (*Shaking off* MOODY'S *arm and saying what is really on his mind.*) If you're vitally interested in my future, prove it! Get me some fights—fights with contenders, not with dumb-bunny club fighters. Get me some main bouts in the metropolitan area ——!

MOODY. (*Losing his temper.*) For a kid who got kayoed five weeks ago, your mouth is pretty big! (*The general bell sounds, the din begins.*)

JOE. That won't happen again! And how about some mention in the press? Twenty-six bouts—no one knows I'm alive. This isn't

40

a vacation for me—it's a profession! I'm staying more than a week. Match me up against real talent You can't go too fast for me. Don't worry about autos!

MOODY. We can go too fast! You're not so good!

JOE. (*With a boyish grin.*) Look at the records! (JOE *abruptly exits.* TOKIO *follows him, first giving the others a glance.*)

MOODY. Boy, oh, boy, that kid's changing!

ROXY. He goes past my head like a cold wind from the river!

LORNA. But you're gettin' what you want—the contender for the crown!

MOODY. I wish I was sure.

ROXY. Frankenstein! (EDDIE FUSELI *saunters down to the others.*)

EDDIE. I thought it over, Tom. I like to get a piece of that boy.

MOODY. (*Angrily.*) I thought it over, too—not for sale. In fact I had a visitation from Jehovah. He came down on the calm waters and He said, "Let there be unity in the ownership."

EDDIE. (*With a dead face.*) I had a visit, too. He come down in the bar and He ate a pretzel. And He says, "Eddie Fuseli, I like you to buy a piece!"

MOODY. (*Trying to delay the inevitable.*) Why not see me in my office tomorrow?

EDDIE. It's a cheap office. I get depressed in that office.

MOODY. (*Finally.*) I can't make any guarantees about the boy.

EDDIE. How do you mean it, Tom?

MOODY. I don't know what the hell he'll do in the next six months.

ROXY. Eddie, it's like flap-jacks—up and down—you don't know which side next!

EDDIE. (*With his small mirthless laugh.*) Ha ha, that's a good one. You oughta be on the radio.

MOODY. No, it's a fact ——

ROXY. We had enough headaches already. He's got a father, but how!

EDDIE. Don't want him to fight?

ROXY. His father sits on the kid's head like a bird's nest! (ROXY *puts his hand on* EDDIE'S *arm.*)

EDDIE. Take your hand off. (ROXY *hastily withdraws.*) Let the boy decide. . . .

MOODY. If you buy in?

EDDIE. Let the boy decide.

MOODY. Sure! But if he says no —— (*Before* MOODY *can finish*

JOE *enters.* EDDIE *whirls around and faces* JOE, *getting his cue from the others. Curiously,* EDDIE *is almost embarrassed before* JOE. *The bell sounds, the din stops.*) Joe, this is Eddie Fuseli. He's a man around town —

EDDIE. (*Facing* JOE, *his back to the others.*) With good connections —

MOODY. He wantsa buy a piece of you —

EDDIE. (*Whirling around.*) I will tell him myself. (*Turning back to* JOE; *with quiet intense dignity.*) I'm Eyetalian too—Eyetalian born, but an American citizen. I like to buy a piece of you. I don't care for no profit. I could turn it back to—*you* could take my share. But I like a good fighter; I like a good boy who could win the crown. It's the in-ter-rest of my life. It would be a proud thing for me when Bonaparte could win the crown like I think he can.

MOODY. (*Confidently.*) It's up to you, Joe, if he buys in.

EDDIE. (*Wooingly.*) Some managers can't give you what you need —

MOODY. Don't say that!

EDDIE. *Some* managers can't! I'll see you get good bouts . . . also press notices . . . I know how. You're a boy who needs that. You decide . . . (*There is a pause,* JOE'S *eyes flit from* LORNA *to the others and back to* EDDIE.)

JOE. Not my half.

EDDIE. Not your half.

JOE. As long as Mr. Fuseli doesn't mix in my private life . . . cut it up any way you like. Excuse me, I got a date with Miss Deusenberg. (*The others silently watch* JOE *exit.*)

EDDIE. A date with who?

MOODY. (*Snorting.*) Miss Deusenberg!

ROXY. An automobile. It gives you an idea what a boy—" Miss Deusenberg " !

EDDIE. How do you like it, Tom? Big bills or little bills?

MOODY. Don't think you're buying in for an apple and an egg.

EDDIE. Take big bills—they're new, they feel good. See you in that office tomorrow. (*The bell clangs off stage.* EDDIE *starts off, but abruptly turns and faces* ROXY *whom he inwardly terrifies.*) It's a trick you don't know, Roxy: when a bird sits on your head and interferes with the championship, you shoot him off. All kinds of birds. You be surprised how fast they fall on the ground.

42

Which is my intention in this syndicate. (*He smiles thinly and then moves out of the scene like a cat.*)

MOODY. I don't like that!

ROXY. I'm not so happy myself at the present time. How do you like it with our boy for gratitude? He leaves us here standing in our brevities!

LORNA. What makes you think you're worthy of gratitude?

MOODY. (*To* LORNA.) For pete's sake, pipe down! Are you with us or against us?

ROXY. (*Haughtily, to* MOODY.) Take my advice, Tom. Marry her and the first year give her a baby. Then she'll sit in the corner and get fat and sleepy, and not have such a big mouth! Uncle Roxy's telling you!

LORNA. (*To* ROXY.) Couldn't you keep quiet about the father to that gunman? Go home and let your wife give *you* a baby!

ROXY. A woman shouldn't interfere ——

MOODY. Peace, for chri' sake, peace! Lorna, we're in a bad spot with Joe. He's getting hard to manage and this is the time when everything's gotta be right. I'm seeing Lombardo's manager tomorrow! Now that gunman's on my tail. You have to help me. You and I wanna do it like the story books, " happy ever after "? Then help me.

LORNA. How?

MOODY. Go after the boy. Keep him away from his folks. Get him away from the buggies ——

LORNA. How?

MOODY. (*Impatiently.*) You know how.

ROXY. Now you're talking.

LORNA. (*Pointing to* ROXY.) You mean the way I see it on his face?

MOODY. For crying out loud! Where do you come off to make a remark like that?

LORNA. You expect me to sleep with that boy?

MOODY. I could tear your ears off for a remark like that!

ROXY. (*Discreetly.*) I think I'll go grab a corn-beef sandwich. (*He exits.*)

MOODY (*After silence.*) Are you mad?

LORNA. (*Tight-lipped.*) No.

MOODY. (*Seductively.*) I'm not a bad guy, Lorna. I don't mean anything bad. . . . All right, I'm crude—sometimes I'm worried and I'm crude. (*The bell clangs, the boxing din stops.*) But what

43

the hell, my heart's in the right place. . . . (*Coming behind her and putting his arms around her as she looks ahead.*) Lorna, don't we both want that sun to come up and shine on us? Don't we? Before you know it the summer'll be here. Then it's the winter again, and it's another year again . . . and we're not married yet. See? . . . See what I mean . . . ?

LORNA. (*Quietly.*) Yes. . . .

MOODY. (*Beaming, but with uncertainty.*) That sounds like the girl I used to know.

LORNA. I see what you mean. . . .

MOODY. (*Worried underneath.*) You're not still mad?

LORNA. (*Briefly.*) I'm not mad. (*But she abruptly cuts out of the scene, leaving* MOODY *standing there.*)

MOODY. (*Shaking his head.*) Boy, I still don't know anything about women . . . !

MEDIUM FADEOUT

ACT II

SCENE 2

A few nights later. Same scene as Act 1, Scene 4. LORNA *and* JOE *sit on same park bench.*

JOE. Some nights I wake up—my heart's beating a mile a minute! Before I open my eyes I know what it is—the feeling that someone's standing at my bed. Then I open my eyes . . . it's gone— ran away!

LORNA. Maybe it's that old fiddle of yours.

JOE. Lorna, maybe it's you. . . .

LORNA. Don't you ever think of it any more—music?

JOE. What're you trying to remind me of? A kid with a Buster Brown collar and a violin case tucked under his arm? Does that sound appetizing to you?

LORNA. Not when you say it that way. You said it different once. . . .

JOE. What's on your mind, Lorna?

LORNA. What's on yours?

JOE. (*Simply.*) You. . . . You're real for me—the way music was real.

LORNA. You've got your car, your career—what do you want with me?

JOE. I develop the ability to knock down anyone my weight. But what point have I made? Don't you think I know that? I went off to the wars 'cause someone called me a name—because I wanted to be two other guys. Now it's happening. . . . I'm not sure I like it.

LORNA. Moody's against that car of yours.

JOE. I'm against Moody, so we're even.

LORNA. Why don't you like him?

JOE. He's a manager! He treats me like a possession! I'm just a little silver mine for him—he bangs me around with a shovel!

LORNA. He's helped you ——

JOE. No, Tokio's helped me. Why don't you give him up? It's terrible to have just a Tuesday-night girl. Why don't you belong to me every night in the week? Why don't you teach me love? . . . Or am I being a fool?

LORNA. You're not a fool, Joe.

JOE. I want you to be my family, my life —— Why don't you do it, Lorna, why?

LORNA. He loves me.

JOE. I love you !

LORNA. (*Treading delicately.*) Well. . . . Anyway, the early bird got the worm. Anyway, I can't give him anguish. I . . . I know what it's like. You shouldn't kick Moody around. He's poor compared to you. You're alive, you've got yourself—I can't feel sorry for you!

JOE. But you don't love him!

LORNA. I'm not much interested in myself. But the thing I like best about you . . . you still feel like a flop. It's mysterious, Joe. It makes me put my hand out. (*She gives him her hand and he grasps it.*)

JOE. I feel very close to you, Lorna.

LORNA. I know. . . .

JOE. And you feel close to me. But you're afraid ——

LORNA. Of what?

JOE. To take a chance! Lorna darling, you won't let me wake

45

you up! I feel it all the time—you're half dead, and you don't know it!

LORNA. (*Half smiling.*) Maybe I do. . . .

JOE. Don't smile—don't be hard-boiled!

LORNA. (*Sincerely.*) I'm not.

JOE. Don't you trust me?

LORNA. (*Evasively.*) Why start what we can't finish?

JOE. (*Fiercely.*) Oh, Lorna, deep as my voice will reach—*listen!* Why can't you leave him? Why?

LORNA. Don't pull my dress off—I hear you.

JOE. Why?

LORNA. Because he needs me and you don't ——

JOE. That's not true!

LORNA. Because he's a desperate guy who always starts out with two strikes against him. Because he's a kid at forty-two and you're a man at twenty-two.

JOE. You're sorry for him?

LORNA. What's wrong with that?

JOE. But what do *you* get?

LORNA. I told you before I don't care.

JOE. I don't believe it!

LORNA. I can't help that!

JOE. What did he ever do for you?

LORNA. (*With sudden verve.*) Would you like to know? He loved me in a world of enemies, of stags and bulls! . . . and I loved him for that. He picked me up in Friskin's hotel on 39th Street. I was nine weeks behind in rent. I hadn't hit the gutter yet, but I was near. He washed my face and combed my hair. He stiffened the space between my shoulder blades. Misery reached out to misery ——

JOE. And now you're dead.

LORNA. (*Lashing out.*) I don't know what the hell you're talking about!

JOE. Yes, you do. . . .

LORNA. (*Withdrawing.*) Ho hum. . . . (*There is silence. The soft park music plays in the distance. The traffic lights change.* LORNA *is trying to appear impassive.* JOE *begins to whistle softly. Finally* LORNA *picks up his last note and continues, he stops. He picks up her note, and after he whistles a few phrases she picks him up again. This whistling duet continues for almost a minute. Then the*

46

traffic lights change again. LORNA, *beginning in a low voice.*) You make me feel too human, Joe. All I want is peace and quiet, not love. I'm a tired old lady, Joe, and I don't mind being what you call " half dead." In fact it's what I like. (*Her voice mounting higher.*) The twice I was in love I took an awful beating and I don't want it again! (*Now half crying.*) I want you to stop it! Don't devil me, Joe. I beg you, don't devil me . . . let me alone. . . . (*She cries softly.* JOE *reaches out and takes her hand, he gives her a handkerchief which she uses.* LORNA, *finally.*) That's the third time I cried in my life. . . .

JOE. Now I know you love me.

LORNA. (*Bitterly.*) Well . . .

JOE. I'll tell Moody.

LORNA. Not yet. Maybe he'd kill you if he knew.

JOE. Maybe.

LORNA. Then Fuseli'd kill him. . . . I guess I'd be left to kill myself. I'll tell him. . . .

JOE. When?

LORNA. Not tonight.

JOE. Swiftly, do it swiftly ——

LORNA. Not tonight.

JOE. Everything's easy if you do it swiftly.

LORNA. He went up there tonight with six hundred bucks to bribe her into divorce.

JOE. Oh . . .

LORNA. (*Sadly.*) He's a good guy, neat all over—sweet. I'll tell him tomorrow. I'd like a drink.

JOE. Let's drive over the Washington Bridge.

LORNA. (*Standing.*) No, I'd like a drink.

JOE. (*Standing and facing her.*) Lorna, when I talk to you . . . something moves in my heart. Gee, it's the beginning of a wonderful life! A man and his girl! A warm living girl who shares your room. . . .

LORNA. Take me home with you.

JOE. Yes.

LORNA. But how do I know you love me?

JOE. Lorna . . .

LORNA. How do I know it's true? You'll get to be the champ. They'll all want you, all the girls! But I don't care! I've been undersea a long time! When they'd put their hands on me I used

47

to say, "This isn't it! This isn't what I mean!" It's been a mysterious world for me! But, Joe, I think you're it! I don't know why, I think you're it! Take me home with you.

JOE. Lorna!

LORNA. Poor Tom . . .

JOE. Poor Lorna! (*The rest is embrace and kiss and clutching each other.*)

SLOW FADEOUT

ACT II

SCENE 3

The next day: the office as in Act 1, Scene 1. LORNA *and* MOODY *are present. She has a hangover and is restless.*

MOODY. Boy, you certainly double-scotched yourself last night. What's the idea, you making a career of drinking in your old age? Headache?

LORNA. No.

MOODY. I won't let you walk alone in the park any more, if you do that.

LORNA. (*Nasty in spite of her best intentions.*) Well, if you stayed away from your wife for a change . . .

MOODY. It's pretty late to bring that up, isn't it? Tuesday nights ——

LORNA. I can't help it—I feel like a tramp. I've felt like a tramp for years.

MOODY. She was pretty friendly last night.

LORNA. Yeah? Did you sleep with her?

MOODY. What the hell's the matter with you, Lorna? (*He goes to her. She shrugs away from him.*)

LORNA. Keep off the grass! (MOODY *gives her a quizzical look, goes back to his desk and from there gives her another quizzical look.*)

MOODY. Why do you drink like that?

LORNA. (*Pointing to her chest.*) Right here—there's a hard lump and I drink to dissolve it. Do you mind?

MOODY. I don't mind—as long as you keep your health.

48

LORNA. Aw, Christ!—you and your health talks!

MOODY. You're looking for a fight, dolly-girl!

LORNA. And you'll give it?

MOODY. (*With a grin.*) No, I'm feeling too good.

LORNA. (*Sitting wearily.*) Who left you a fortune?

MOODY. Better. Monica's seen the light. The truth is she's begun to run around with a retired brewer and now *she* wants the divorce.

LORNA. Good, now she can begin paying you.

MOODY. She goes to Reno in a few months.

LORNA. (*Moodily.*) I feel like a tramp. . . .

MOODY. That's what I'm telling you —— In a few months we'll be married! (*He laughs with pleasure.*)

LORNA. You still want to marry me? Don't I feel like an old shoe to you?

MOODY. (*Coming to her.*) Honest, you're so dumb!

LORNA. (*Touched by his boyishness.*) You're so sweet. . . .

MOODY. And flash!—I signed Lombardo today! They meet six weeks from tonight.

LORNA. Goody. . . .

MOODY. (*Disappointed by her flippant reaction, but continuing.*) I'm still not sure what he'll show with Lombardo. But my present worry is this: help me get that kid straight. Did you speak to him about the driving last night?

LORNA. I didn't see him. . . .

MOODY. It's very important. A Lombardo win clinches everything. In the fall we ride up to the Chocolate's door and dump him in the gutter! After that . . . I don't like to exaggerate—but the kid's primed! And you and I—Lorna baby, we're set. (*Happily.*) What do you think of that?

LORNA. (*Evasively.*) You draw beautiful pictures. (*A knock sounds on the door.*)

MOODY. Come in. (SIGGIE *enters, dressed in cab driver's garb.*)

SIGGIE. Hello, Miss Moon.

LORNA. Hello. You know Mr. Moody.

SIGGIE. (*To* MOODY.) Hello.

MOODY. What can we do for you?

SIGGIE. For me you can't do nothing. I'm sore. I'm here against my better instinct. (*Taking a roll of money from his pocket and slapping it on desk.*) He don't want it—no part of it! My father-in-law don't want it. Joe sent it up—two hundred bucks—enough to choke a horse—but he don't want it!

MOODY. Why?

LORNA. That's nice he remembers his folks.

SIGGIE. Listen, I got a father-in-law nothing's nice to him but feeding his horse and giving a laugh and slicing philosophical salami across the table! He's sore because Joe don't come home half the time. As a matter of fact, ain't he suppose to come to sleep no more? The old man's worried.

MOODY. That's not my concern.

SIGGIE. I can't see what it's such a worry. A boy gets in the higher brackets—what's the worry? He's got enough clothes now to leave three suits home in the closet. (*Turning to* LORNA.) It won't hurt if he sends me a few passes—tell him I said so.

LORNA. How's the wife?

SIGGIE. The Duchess? Still laughing.

LORNA. When you getting that cab?

SIGGIE. Do me a favor, Miss Moon—tell him I could use this wad for the first instalment.

LORNA. I'll tell him. Tell Mr. Bonaparte I saw Joe last night. He's fine.

MOODY. I'll see you get some passes.

SIGGIE. Thanks, thanks to both of you. Adios. (*He exits.*)

LORNA. He and his wife are crazy for each other. Married . . . they throw each other around, but they're like love birds. Marriage is something special. . . . I guess you have to deserve it.

MOODY. I thought you didn't see Joe last night.

LORNA. I didn't, but why worry his father?

MOODY. The hell with his father.

LORNA. The hell with you!

MOODY. (*After a brooding pause.*) I'll tell you something, Lorna. I'm not overjoyed the way Joe looks at you.

LORNA. How's he look?

MOODY. As if he saw the whole island of Manhattan in your face, and I don't like it.

LORNA. You thought of that too late.

MOODY. Too late for what?

LORNA. To bawl me out.

MOODY. Who's bawling you out?

LORNA. You were about to. Or warn me. I don't need warnings.

(*Coasting away from the argument.*) If you saw Joe's father you'd like him.

MOODY. I saw him.

LORNA. If you knew him you'd like him.

MOODY. Who wantsa like him? What do I need him for? I don't like him and I don't like his son! It's a business—Joe does his work, I do mine. Like this telephone—I pay the bill and I use it!

LORNA. He's human. . . .

MOODY. What're we fighting about?

LORNA. We're fighting about love. I'm trying to tell you how cynical I am. Tell the truth, love doesn't last ——

MOODY. (*Suddenly quietly serious.*) Everything I said about Joe— the opposite goes for you. Love lasts . . . if you want it to. . . . I want it to last. I need it to last. What the hell's all this struggle to make a living for if not for a woman and a home? I don't kid myself. I know what I need. I need you, Lorna.

LORNA. It has to end. . . .

MOODY. What has to end?

LORNA. Everything.

MOODY. What're you talking about?

LORNA. I oughta burn. I'm leaving you. . . .

MOODY. (*With a sick smile.*) That's what you think.

LORNA. (*Not looking at him.*) I mean it.

MOODY. (*As above.*) I mean it too.

LORNA. (*After looking at him for a moment.*) You can't take a joke?

MOODY. (*Not knowing where he stands.*) It all depends. . . . I don't like a joke that pushes the blood down in my feet.

LORNA. (*Coming to him and putting her arms around his neck.*) That's true, you're pale.

MOODY. Who's the man?

LORNA. (*Heartsick, and unable to tell him the truth.*) There's no man, Tom . . . even if there was, I couldn't leave you. (*She looks at him, unable to say more.*)

MOODY. (*After a pause.*) How about some lunch? I'll buy it. . . .

LORNA. (*Wearily.*) Where would I put it, Tom?

MOODY. (*Impulsively.*) In your hat! (*And suddenly he embraces her roughly and kisses her fully and she allows it. JOE walks into office, EDDIE FUSELI behind him. They break apart.*)

51

JOE. The first time I walked in here that was going on. It's one long duet around here.

MOODY. Hello.

EDDIE. (*Sardonically.*) Hello, Partner. . . . (LORNA *is silent and avoids* JOE'S *looks.*)

JOE. How about that fight with Lombardo?

MOODY. Six weeks from tonight.

JOE. He's gonna be surprised.

MOODY. (*Coolly.*) No one doubts it.

JOE. (*Sharply.*) I didn't say it was doubted!

MOODY. Boy, everyone's off his feed today. It started with the elevator boy—next it's Lorna—now it's you! What are *you* sore about?

LORNA. (*Trying to turn the conversation, to* JOE.) Siggie was here looking for you. Your father's worried ——

JOE. Not as much as my " manager " worries me.

MOODY. I don't need you to tell me how to run my business. I'll book the matches ——

JOE. That doesn't worry me.

MOODY. But you and your speeding worries me! First it's music, then it's motors. Christ, next it'll be girls and booze!

JOE. It's girls already.

LORNA. Joe ——

JOE. (*Bitterly.*) Certainly! By the dozens!

EDDIE. Haha—that's a hot one. Don't ask me which is worst—women or spiders.

LORNA. Siggie left this money—your father won't take it. Siggie says buy him a cab —— (JOE *takes money.*)

EDDIE. Your relative? I'll get him a cab. (*To* MOODY.) How about a flock of bouts for Bonaparte over the summer?

MOODY. (*Bitterly.*) All he wants—practice fights—to make him a better " artiste."

EDDIE. That is what we like. (JOE *is looking at* LORNA.)

MOODY. " We? " Where do I come in?

EDDIE. You push the buttons, the *right* buttons. I wanna see Bonaparte with the crown.

MOODY. (*Sarcastically.*) Your concern touches me deep in my heart!

EDDIE. What's the matter, Tom? You getting tired?

MOODY. (*Coolly.*) I get tired, don't you?

EDDIE. Don't get tired, Tom . . . not in a crucial time.

MOODY. Get him to give up that Deusenberg.

EDDIE. (*After looking at* JOE.) That's his fun. . . .

MOODY. His fun might cost your crown.

JOE. (*Suddenly, to* LORNA.) Why did you kiss him?

MOODY. (*To* JOE.) It's about time you shut your mouth and minded your own goddam business. Also, that you took some orders.

JOE. (*Suddenly savage.*) Who are you, God?

MOODY. Yes! I'm your maker, you cock-eyed gutter rat! Outa sawdust and spit I made you! I own you—without me you're a blank! Your insolence is gorgeous, but this is the end! I'm a son of a gun! What're you so superior about?

EDDIE. Don't talk so quick, Tom. You don't know . . .

MOODY. I wouldn't take the crap of this last six-eight months from the President himself! Cut me up in little pieces, baby—but not me!

EDDIE. (*Quietly.*) You could get cut up in little pieces.

MOODY. (*Retiring in disgust.*) Sisst!

EDDIE. You hear me?

MOODY. (*From his desk.*) You wanna manage this boy? Help yourself—do it! I'll sell my piece for half of what it's worth. You wanna buy?

EDDIE. You are a funny man.

MOODY. Gimme twenty thousand and lemme out. Ten, I'll take ten. I got my girl. I don't need crowns or jewels. I take my girl and we go sit by the river and it's everything.

JOE. What girl?

MOODY. I'm not on speaking terms with you! (*To* EDDIE.) Well?

EDDIE. It would be funny if your arms got broke.

JOE. Wait a minute! Lorna loves me and I love her.

MOODY. (*After looking from* JOE *to* LORNA *and back.*) Crazy as a bat! (*He laughs.*)

JOE. (*Frigidly.*) Is it so impossible?

MOODY. About as possible as hell freezes over. (*He and* JOE *simultaneously turn to* LORNA.)

JOE. Tell him. . . .

LORNA. (*Looking* JOE *in the face.*) I love Tom. Tell him what?

(JOE *looks at her intently. Silence.* JOE *then turns and quietly exits from the office.* MOODY *shakes his head with a grin.*)

MOODY. Eddie, I take everything back. I was a fool to get sore— that boy's a real nutsy-Fagan! (*He offers his hand.* EDDIE *looks at it and then viciously slaps it down.*)

EDDIE. (*Repressing a trembling voice.*) I don't like no one to laugh at that boy. You call a boy like that a rat? An educated boy? What is your idea to call him cock-eyed? When you do it in front of me, I say, " Tom don't like himself " . . . for Bonaparte is a good friend to me . . . you're a clever manager for him. That's the only reason I take your slop. Do your business, Tom. (*To* LORNA.) And that goes for you, too! No tricks, Miss Moon!

(*He slowly exits.* MOODY *stands there thoughtfully.* LORNA *moves to couch.*)

MOODY. I'm a son of a gun!

LORNA. I feel like I'm shot from a cannon.

MOODY. Why?

LORNA. I'm sorry for him.

MOODY. Why? Because he's a queer?

LORNA. I'm not talking of Fuseli. (*Suddenly* LORNA'S *eyes flood with tears.* MOODY *takes her hand, half sensing the truth.*)

MOODY. What's wrong, Lorna? You can tell me. . . .

LORNA. I feel like the wrath of God.

MOODY. You like that boy, don't you?

LORNA. I love him, Tom.

SLOW FADEOUT

ACT II

SCENE 4

Six weeks later.
A dressing room [1] *before the Lombardo fight. There are a couple of rubbing tables in the room. There are some lockers and a few hooks on which hang pieces of clothing. A door to the left leads to the showers; a door to the right leads to the arena.*
As the lights fade in, BONAPARTE *and* SIGGIE *are sitting*

[1] See Production Notes, p. 4.

to one side, on a long wooden bench. TOKIO *is fussing around in a locker. A fighter,* PEPPER WHITE, *hands already bandaged, is being rubbed down by his trainer-manager,* MICKEY. *Throughout the scene is heard the distant roar of* THE CROWD *and the clanging of the bell.*[1]

BONAPARTE. (*After a silence of intense listening.*) What is that noise?

SIGGIE. That's the roar of the crowd.

BONAPARTE. A thousand people?

SIGGIE. Six thousand.

PEPPER WHITE. (*Turning his head as he lies on his belly.*) Nine thousand.

SIGGIE. That's right, nine. You're sitting under nine thousand people. Suppose they fell down on your head? Did you ever think of that? (*The outside door opens,* EDDIE FUSELI *enters. The distant bell clangs.* EDDIE *looks around suspiciously, then asks* TOKIO:)

EDDIE. Where's Bonaparte?

TOKIO. Still with the newspapermen.

EDDIE. (*Unpleasantly surprised.*) He's what?

TOKIO. Tom took him upstairs—some sports writers.

EDDIE. A half hour before a fight? What is Moody trying to do?

TOKIO. Tom's the boss.

EDDIE. Looka, Tokio—in the future you are gonna take your orders from me! (*Pointing to* SIGGIE *and* BONAPARTE.) Who is this?

TOKIO. Joe's relatives.

EDDIE. (*Going over to them.*) Is this his father?

BONAPARTE. (*Somberly.*) Yes, thisa his father.

SIGGIE. And this is his brother-in-law. Joe sent passes up the house. We just got here. I thought it was in Coney Island—it's lucky I looked at the tickets. Believe it or not, the old man never seen a fight in his life! Is it human?

EDDIE. (*Coldly.*) Shut your mouth a minute! This is The Arena—Bonaparte is fighting a good man tonight ——

SIGGIE. Ahh, that Lombardo's a bag of oats!

EDDIE. When Bonaparte goes in there I like him to have one thing on his mind—fighting! I hope you understand me. An' I don't like to find you here when I return! I hope you understand that. . . .

[1] See copyright page for data on sound effect records.

(After a full glance at them EDDIE *gracefully exits.)*

SIGGIE. That's a positive personality!

TOKIO. That's Eddie Fuseli.

SIGGIE. Momma-mia! No wonder I smelled gunpowder! *(Turning to* BONAPARTE.*)* Pop, that's a paradox in human behavior: he shoots you for a nickel—then for fifty bucks he sends you flowers!

TOKIO. *(Referring to distant bell.)* That's the next bout.

SIGGIE. *(To* BONAPARTE.*)* Come on, we don't wanna miss the whole show.

BONAPARTE. I waita for Joe.

SIGGIE. You heard what Fuseli said ——

BONAPARTE. *(With somber stubbornness.)* I gonna wait!

SIGGIE. Listen, pop, you ——

BONAPARTE. *(With sudden force.)* I say I gonna wait!!

SIGGIE. *(Handing* BONAPARTE *a ticket.)* Ticket. *(Shrugging.)* Good-bye, you're letting flies in! *(*SIGGIE *exits jauntily.* BONAPARTE *silently watches* TOKIO *work over the fighter's materials. A* SECOND *comes in, puts a pail under table where* TOKIO *hovers, and exits.* PEPPER WHITE, *his head turned, watches* BONAPARTE *as he hums a song.)*

PEPPER.

Oh, Sweet Dardanella, I love your harem eyes,

Oh, Sweet Dardanella, I'm a lucky fellow to get such a prize. . . . *(To* BONAPARTE.*)* So you're Bonaparte's little boy, Buddy? Why didn't you say so before? Come over here and shake my hand. *(*BONAPARTE *does so.)* Tell Bonaparte I like to fight him.

BONAPARTE. Why?

PEPPER. I like to beat him up.

BONAPARTE. *(Naively, not amused.)* Why? You don't like him?

PEPPER. Don't kid me, Buddy! *(A* CALL BOY *looks in at the door.)*

CALL BOY. Pepper White! Ready, Pepper White! *(*CALL BOY *exits.* PEPPER WHITE *slips off table and begins to change his shoes.)*

PEPPER. *(To* BONAPARTE.*)* When I get back I'll explain you all the ins and outs. *(A* SECOND *enters, takes a pail from* MICKEY *and exits.* LORNA *enters.* PEPPER, *indignantly.)* Who told girls to come in here?!

LORNA. Modest? Close your eyes. Is Moody . . . ? *(Suddenly seeing* BONAPARTE.*)* Hello, Mr. Bonaparte!

56

BONAPARTE. (*Glad to see a familiar face.*) Hello, hello, Missa Moon! Howa you feel?

LORNA. What brings you to this part of the world?

BONAPARTE. (*Somberly.*) I come-a to see Joe. . . .

LORNA. Why, what's wrong?

BONAPARTE. (*With a slow shrug.*) He don't come-a to see me. . . .

LORNA. Does he know you're here?

BONAPARTE. No. (LORNA *looks at him sympathetically.*)

LORNA. (*Finally.*) It's a three-ring circus, isn't it?

BONAPARTE. How you mean?

LORNA. Oh, I mean you . . . and him . . . and other people . . .

BONAPARTE. I gonna see how he fight.

LORNA. I owe you a report. I wish I had good news for you, but I haven't.

BONAPARTE. Yes, I know . . . he gotta wild wolf inside—eat him up!

LORNA. You could build a city with his ambition to be somebody.

BONAPARTE. (*Sadly, shaking his head.*) No . . . burn down!

(*Now the outside door is thrust open—the distant bell clangs. JOE enters, behind him MOODY and ROXY. JOE stops in his tracks when he sees LORNA and his father together—the last two persons in the world he wants to see now. His hands are already bandaged, a bathrobe is thrown around his shoulders.*)

JOE. Hello, poppa. . . .

BONAPARTE. Hello, Joe. . . .

JOE. (*Turning to TOKIO.*) Throw out the girls—this isn't a hotel bedroom!

MOODY. That's no way to talk!

JOE. (*Coolly.*) I talk as I please!

MOODY. (*Angrily.*) The future Mrs. Moody ——

JOE. I don't want her here!

LORNA. He's right, Tom. Why fight about it? (*She exits.*)

JOE. (*To* MOODY.) Also, I don't want to see writers again before a fight; it makes me nervous!

ROXY. (*Softly, for a wonder.*) They're very important, Joe ——

JOE. I'm important! My mind must be clear before I fight. I have to think before I go in. Don't you know that yet?

57

ROXY. (*Suddenly.*) Yeah, we know—you're a stoodent—you gotta look in your notes.

JOE. What's funny about that? I do, *I do!*

ROXY. (*Retreating.*) So I said you do! (PEPPER WHITE *comes forward, about to exit, to* MOODY.)

PEPPER. How 'bout a bout with Napoleon?

MOODY. On your way, louse!

PEPPER. (*With a grin.*) Pickin' setups? (JOE *suddenly turns and starts for* PEPPER. TOKIO *quickly steps in between the two boys.*)

TOKIO. Save it for the ring! (*The two fighters glare at each other. JOE slowly turns and starts back for the table.*)

PEPPER. You think he'll be the champ? Where'd you ever read about a cock-eyed champ? (JOE *spins around, speeds across the room*—PEPPER *is on the floor!* MICKEY *now starts for* JOE. TOKIO *starts for* MICKEY. PEPPER *gets up off floor and finds himself occupied with* MOODY. *For a moment the fight is general.* EDDIE FUSELI *enters. All see him. The fighting magically stops on the second.*)

EDDIE. What'sa matter? Cowboys and Indians? (*To* PEPPER.) Out! (MICKEY *and* PEPPER *sullenly exit. To* MOODY.) I'm lookin' for you! You're a manager and a half! You and your fat friend! (*Meaning* ROXY.) You think this boy is a toy?

JOE. Eddie's the only one here who understands me.

MOODY. Who the hell wantsa understand you! I got one wish—for Lombardo to give you the business! The quicker he taps you off tonight, the better! You gotta be took down a dozen pegs! I'm versus you! Completely versus!

EDDIE. (*Quietly, to* MOODY.) Moody, your brains is in your feet! This is how you handle a coming champ, to give him the jitters before a bout? Go out and take some air! . . . (*Seeing* EDDIE'S *quiet deadliness,* MOODY *swallows his wrath and exits;* ROXY *follows with pursed lips.*)

EDDIE. Lay down, Joe—take it easy. (JOE *sits on a table.*) Who hurt you, Joe? Someone hurt your feelings?

JOE. Everything's all right.

EDDIE. Tokio, I put fifty bucks on Bonaparte's nose for you. It's my appreciation to you. . . .

TOKIO. Thanks.

EDDIE. (*Of* BONAPARTE.) Whatta you want me to do with him?

JOE. Leave him here.

EDDIE. Tell me if you want something. . . .

JOE. Nothing.

EDDIE. Forget that Miss Moon. Stop lookin' down her dress. Go out there and kill Lombardo! Send him out to Woodlawn! Tear his skull off! . . . as I know Bonaparte can do it! (EDDIE *gives* BONAPARTE *a sharp look and exits. There is silence intensified by the distant clang of the bell and the muted roar of* THE CROWD. TOKIO *looks over at* BONAPARTE *who has been silently seated on bench all this time.*)

JOE. (*Not quite knowing what to say.*) How is Anna, poppa?

BONAPARTE. Fine.

JOE. Siggie watching the fights?

BONAPARTE. Yes. . . .

JOE. You look fine. . . .

BONAPARTE. Yes, feela good. . . .

JOE. Why did you send that money back? (*There is no answer.*) Why did you come here? . . . You sit there like my conscience. . . .

BONAPARTE. Why you say so?

JOE. Poppa, I have to fight, no matter what you say or think! This is my profession! I'm out for fame and fortune, not to be different or artistic! I don't intend to be ashamed of my life!

BONAPARTE. (*Standing up.*) Yeah, I understanda you. . . .

JOE. Go out and watch the fights.

BONAPARTE. (*Somberly.*) Yeah . . . you fight. Now I know . . . is'a too late for music. The men musta be free an' happy for music . . . not like-a you. Now I see whatta you are . . . I give-a you every word to fight . . . I sorry for you. . . . (*Silence. The distant roar of* THE CROWD *climbs up and falls down, the bell clangs again.*)

TOKIO. (*Gently.*) I'll have to ask you to leave, Mr. Bonaparte. . . .

BONAPARTE. (*Holding back his tears.*) Joe . . . I hope-a you win every fight. (BONAPARTE *slowly exits. As he opens and closes the door the roar of* THE CROWD *swells up for an instant.*)

TOKIO. Lay down, Joe. There's five minutes left to tune you up.

JOE. (*In a low voice.*) That's right, tune me up. . . . (JOE *stretches out on his stomach and* TOKIO'S *busy hands start up the back of his legs.*)

TOKIO. (*Working with steady briskness.*) I never worried less about a boy . . . in my life. You're a real sweetheart. . . .

(*Suddenly* JOE *begins to cry in his arms.* TOKIO *looks down, momentarily hesitates in his work—then slowly goes ahead with his massaging hands. The* BOY *continues to shake with silent sobs. Again the bell clangs in the distance. In a soft caressing voice.*)

You're getting good, honey. Maybe I never told you that before. I seen it happen before. (*Continuing the massaging.*) It seems to happen sudden—a fighter gets good. He gets easy and graceful. He learns how to save himself—no energy wasted . . . he slips and slides—he travels with the punch. . . . Oh, sure, I like the way you're shaping up. (TOKIO *continues massaging.* JOE *is silent. His sobbing stops. After a moment* TOKIO *continues.*) What was you saying about Lombardo's trick? I understood you to say he's a bull's-eye for a straight shot from the inside. I think you're right, Joe, but that kind of boy is liable to meet you straight-on in a clinch and give you the back of his head under the chin. Watch out for that.

JOE. He needs a straight punch. . . . (JOE *suddenly sits up on table, his legs dangling.*) Now I'm alone. They're all against me—Moody, the girl . . . you're my family now, Tokio—you and Eddie! I'll show them all—nobody stands in my way! My father's had his hand on me for years. No more. No more for her either—she had her chance! When a bullet sings through the air it has no past—only a future—like me! Nobody, nothing stands in my way! (*In a sudden spurt of feeling* JOE *starts sparring around lightly in a shadow boxing routine.* TOKIO *smiles with satisfaction. Now the roar of* THE CROWD *reaches a frenzied shriek and hangs there. The bell clangs rapidly several times. The roar of* THE CROWD *settles down again.*)

TOKIO. That sounds like the kill. (JOE *draws his bathrobe around him and prances on his toes.*)

JOE. I'm a new boy tonight! I could take two Lombardos! (*Vigorously shaking out his bandaged hands above his head.*) Hallelujah! We're on the Millionaire Express tonight! Nobody gets me! (*The door is thrust open and a* CALL BOY *shouts.*)

CALL BOY. Bonaparte, ready. Bonaparte, ready. (PEPPER WHITE *and* MICKY *enter as the* CALL BOY *speeds away.* PEPPER *is flushed with victory.*)

PEPPER. (*To* JOE.) Tell me when you want it; you can have it the way I just give it to Pulaski! (JOE *looks* PEPPER *in the face, flexes his hands several times and suddenly breaks out in laughter, to* PEPPER'S *astonishment.* JOE *and* TOKIO *exit.* PEPPER *throws off his robe and displays his body.*) Look me over—not a mark. How do you like that for class! I'm in a hurry to grab a cab to Flushing.

MICKEY. (*Impassively.*) Keep away from her.

PEPPER. I don't even hear you.

MICKEY. Keep away from her!

PEPPER. I go for her like a bee and the flower.

MICKEY. (*In a droning prophetic voice.*) The flower is married. Her husband is an excitable Armenian from the Orient. There will be hell to pay! Keep away from her! (*Now in the distance is heard the indistinct high voice of the announcer.*)

PEPPER. You oughta get me a fight with that cock-eye Napoleon—insteada sticking your nose where it don't belong! I could slaughter him in next to nothing.

MICKEY. (*Impassively.*) If you could make his weight and slaughter him, you'd be the next world's champ. But you can't make his weight, you can't slaughter him, and you can't be the champ. Why the hell don't you take a shower? (*The bell clangs—in the arena,* JOE'S *fight is on.*)

PEPPER. (*Plaintively, beginning to dress at his locker.*) If my girl don't like me without a shower, I'll tell her a thing or two.

MICKEY. If her husband don't tell you first. (*The roar of* THE CROWD *swells up as the door opens and* BONAPARTE *enters. He is unusually agitated. He looks at* PEPPER *and* MICKEY *and sits on a bench. The roar of* THE CROWD *mounts higher than before, then drops.*)

PEPPER. (*To* BONAPARTE.) What's the matter with you?

BONAPARTE. (*Shaking his head.*) Don't like to see . . .

PEPPER. (*Delighted.*) Why? Your boy gettin' smeared?

BONAPARTE. They fighta for money, no?

MICKEY. No, they're fighting for a noble cause ——

BONAPARTE. If they wasa fight for cause or for woman, woulda not be so bad.

PEPPER. (*Still dressing behind locker door.*) I fight for money and I like it. I don't fight for under a thousand bucks. Do I, Mickey?

MICKEY. Nope.

PEPPER. (*Boasting naively.*) I didn't fight for under a thousand for five years. Did I, Mickey?

MICKEY. (*Impassively.*) Nope.

61

PEPPER. I get a thousand bucks tonight, don't I?

MICKEY. Nope.

PEPPER. (Up like a shot.) How much? How much tonight?

MICKEY. Twelve hundred bucks.

PEPPER. What? Mickey, I oughta bust you in the nose. How many times do I have to say I don't fight for under one thousand bucks! (To BONAPARTE.) Now you see what I'm up against with this manager!

MICKEY. (Impassively.) Okay, you'll get a thousand.

PEPPER. I better, Buddy! That's all I say—I better! (To BONA-PARTE.) I tell him I want to fight your kid and he don't lift a finger. (The roar of THE CROWD crescendoes and drops down again.)

MICKEY. You don't rate no fight with Bonaparte. (To BONAPARTE, of PEPPER.) He's an old man, a fossil!

BONAPARTE. Who?

MICKEY. Him—he's twenty-nine.

BONAPARTE. Old?

MICKEY. In this business, twenty-nine is ancient.

PEPPER. My girl don't think so.

MICKEY. Keep away from her. (The roar of THE CROWD mounts up to a devilish shriek.)

PEPPER. Wow, is your boy getting schlocked!

BONAPARTE. My boy isa win.

PEPPER. Yeah, and that's why you ran away?

BONAPARTE. Whatta the difference who's-a win? Is terrible to see!

PEPPER. (Grinning.) If I wasn't in a hurry, I'd wait around to help pick up your little Joie's head off the floor. (He draws on a sport shirt.)

MICKEY. (To PEPPER.) What are you wearing a polo shirt on a winter night for?

PEPPER. For crying out loud, I just bought it! . . . So long, Mr. Bonaparte.

BONAPARTE. I aska you please—whatta happen to a boy's hands when he fight a longa time?

PEPPER. (Holding up his fists.) Take a look at mine—I got a good pair. See those knuckles? Flat!

BONAPARTE. Broke?

PEPPER. Not broke, flat!—pushed down!

BONAPARTE. Hurt?

62

PEPPER. You get used to it.

BONAPARTE. Can you use them?

PEPPER. Go down the hall and look at Pulaski.

BONAPARTE. Can you open thees-a hands?

PEPPER. What for?

BONAPARTE. (*Gently touching the fists.*) So strong, so hard. . . .

PEPPER. You said it, Buddy. So long, Buddy. (*To* MICKEY.) Take my stuff.

MICKEY. Sam'll take it after. Keep away from her. (PEPPER *looks at* MICKEY *with a sardonic grin and exits followed by* MICKEY.)

BONAPARTE. (*To himself.*) So strong . . . so useless . . . (*The roar of* THE CROWD *mounts up and calls for a kill.* BONAPARTE *trembles. For a moment he sits quietly on the bench. Then he goes to the door of the shower room and looks around at the boxing paraphernalia. In the distance the bell begins to clang repeatedly.* BONAPARTE *stares in the direction of the arena. He goes to the exit door. The crowd is cheering and howling.* BONAPARTE *hesitates a moment at the door and then rapidly walks back to the bench, where he sits. Head cocked, he listens for a moment. The roar of* THE CROWD *is heated, demanding and hateful. Suddenly* BONAPARTE *jumps to his feet. He is in a murderous mood. He shakes his clenched fist in the direction of the noise—he roars aloud. The roar of* THE CROWD *dies down. The door opens,* PEPPER'S *second,* SAM, *enters, softly whistling to himself. Deftly he begins to sling together* PEPPER'S *paraphernalia.*) What'sa happen in the fight?

SAM. Knockout.

BONAPARTE. Who?

SAM. Lombardo's stiff. (BONAPARTE *slowly sits. Softly whistling,* SAM *exits with the paraphernalia. The outside door is flung open. In come* JOE, TOKIO, MOODY *and* ROXY, *who is elated beyond sanity.* JOE'S *eyes glitter, his face is hard and flushed. He has won by a knockout.*)

ROXY. (*Almost dancing.*) My boy! My darling boy! My dear darling boy! (*Silently* JOE *sits on the edge of the table, ignoring his father after a glance. His robe drops from his shoulders.* ROXY *turns to* MOODY.) How do you like it, Tom? He knocks him out in two rounds!

MOODY. (*Stiffly, to* JOE.) It's good business to call the sports writers in ——

63

ROXY. That's right, give a statement! (MOODY *gives* JOE *a rapid glance and hurriedly exits.*) I'm collecting a bet on you. All my faith and patience is rewarded. (*As he opens the door he almost knocks over* EDDIE FUSELI.) Haha! How do you like it, Eddie? Haha! (*He exits.* EDDIE FUSELI *closes the door and stands with his back to it.* TOKIO *moves up to* JOE *and begins to remove a glove.*)

TOKIO. (*Gently.*) You're a real sweetheart. . . . (TOKIO *removes the sweaty glove and begins to fumble with the lace of the other one.* JOE *carefully moves this glove out of* TOKIO'S *reach, resting it on his opposite arm.*)

JOE. (*Almost proudly.*) Better cut it off. . . . (BONAPARTE *is watching tensely.* EDDIE *watches from the door.*)

TOKIO. . . . Broke? . . .

JOE. (*Holding the hand out proudly.*) Yes, it's broke. . . . (TOKIO *slowly reaches for a knife. He begins carefully to cut the glove.*) Hallelujah!! It's the beginning of the world! (BONAPARTE, *lips compressed, slowly turns his head away.* EDDIE *watches with inner excitement and pleasure,* JOE *has become a fighter.* TOKIO *continues with his work.* JOE *begins to laugh loudly, victoriously, exultantly—with a deep thrill of satisfaction.*)

SLOW FADEOUT

ACT III

SCENE 1

MOODY'S *office, same as Act 1, Scene 1, six months later. Present are* MOODY, *acting the persuasive salesman with two sports writers,* DRAKE *and* LEWIS; ROXY GOTTLIEB *being helpful in his usual manner,* TOKIO, *to one side, characteristically quiet . . . and* JOE BONAPARTE. JOE *sits on desk and diffidently swings his legs as he eats a sandwich. His success has added a certain bellicosity to his attitude, it has changed his clothing to silk shirts and custom-made suits.*

MOODY. He's got his own style. He won't rush ——

ROXY. Nobody claims our boy's Niagara Falls.

DRAKE. (*A newspaperman for twenty years.*) Except himself!

MOODY. You newspaper boys are right.

DRAKE. We newspaper boys are always right!

MOODY. He won't take chances tomorrow night if he can help it. He'll study his man, pick out flaws—then shoot at them.

JOE. (*Casually.*) It won't matter a helluva lot if I win late in the bout or near the opening. The main thing with Bonaparte is to win.

DRAKE. (*Dryly.*) Well, what does Bonaparte expect to do tomorrow night?

JOE. (*As dryly.*) Win.

MOODY. Why shouldn't we have a win from the Chocolate Drop? Look at our record! ——

LEWIS. (*Good-natured and slow.*) We just wanna get an impression ——

MOODY. Seventeen knockouts? Fulton, Lombardo, Guffy Talbot ——?

JOE. Phil Weiner . . .

MOODY. Weiner?

65

ROXY. That's no powderpuff hitter!

LEWIS. In this fight tomorrow night, can you name the round?

JOE. Which round would you like?

DRAKE. You're either a genius or an idiot!

MOODY. Joe don't mean ——

DRAKE. (*Sharply.*) Let him talk for himself.

JOE. (*Getting off the desk.*) Listen, Drake, I'm not the boy I used to be—the honeymoon's over. I don't blush and stammer these days. Bonaparte goes in and slugs with the best. In the bargain his brain is *better* than the best. That's the truth; why deny it?

DRAKE. The last time you met Chocolate you never even touched him!

JOE. It's almost two years since I " never even touched him." Now I know how!

MOODY. What Joe means to say ——

DRAKE. He's the genuine and only modest cock-eyed wonder!

JOE. What good is modesty? I'm a fighter! The whole essence of prizefighting is immodesty! " I'm better than you are—I'll prove it by breaking your face in!" What do you expect? A conscience and a meek smile? I don't believe that bull the meek'll inherit the earth!

DRAKE. Oh, so it's the earth you want!

JOE. I know what I want—that's my business! But I don't want your guff!

DRAKE. I have two sons of my own—I like boys. But I'm a son-of-a-bitch if I can stomach your conceit!

MOODY. (*Trying to save the situation.*) They serve a helluva rum Collins across the street ——

DRAKE. Bonaparte, I'll watch for Waterloo with more than interest.

MOODY. Why don't we run across for a drink? How 'bout some drinks?

DRAKE. Tom, you can buy me twenty drinks and I still won't change my mind about him. (*He exits.*)

LEWIS. (*Smiling.*) You're all right, Bonaparte.

JOE. Thanks. . . .

LEWIS. (*Clinching a cigarette at desk.*) How's that big blonde of yours, Tom?

MOODY. Fine.

LEWIS. How does she feel about the wedding bells? Sunday is it?

(*This is news to* JOE, *and* MOODY *knows it is.*)

MOODY. (*Nervously.*) Happy, the way I am. Yeah, Sunday.

ROXY. How about the drinks? We'll drink to everybody's health!

LEWIS. (*To* JOE.) Good luck tomorrow.

JOE. Thanks. . . . (*They exit,* MOODY *throwing a resentful look at* JOE. JOE *and* TOKIO *are left. In the silence* JOE *goes back to the remains of his lunch.*)

TOKIO. That Drake is a case.

JOE. (*Pushing food away.*) They don't make cheesecake the way they used to when I was a boy. Or maybe I don't like it any more. When are they getting married?

TOKIO. Moody? Sunday.

JOE. Those writers hate me.

TOKIO. You give them too much lip.

JOE. (*Looking down at his clenched fists.*) I'd rather give than take it. That's one reason I became a fighter. When did Moody get his divorce?

TOKIO. Few weeks ago. . . . (*Cannily.*) Why don't you forget Lorna?

JOE. (*As if not understanding.*) What?

TOKIO. I'll say it again . . . why not forget her? (*No answer comes.*) Joe, you're loaded with love. Find something to give it to. Your heart ain't in fighting . . . your *hate* is. But a man with hate and nothing else . . . he's half a man . . . and half a man . . . is no man. Find something to love, or someone. Am I stepping on your toes?

JOE. (*Coldly.*) I won't be unhappy if you mind your business.

TOKIO. Okay. . . . (TOKIO *goes to door, stops there.*) Watch your dinner tonight. No girls either.

JOE. Excuse me for saying that ——

TOKIO. (*With a faint smile.*) Okay. (TOKIO *opens door and* LORNA MOON *enters.* TOKIO *smiles at her and exits. She carries a pack of newspapers under her arm.* JOE *and she do not know what to say to each other—they wish they had not met here.* LORNA *crosses and puts newspapers on desk. She begins to bang through desk drawers, looking for scissors.*)

JOE. I hear you're making the leap tomorrow. . .

LORNA. Sunday. . . .

JOE. Sunday. (*Intense silence.*)

67

LORNA. (*To say anything.*) I'm looking for the scissors. . . .

JOE. Who're you cutting up today?

LORNA. (*Bringing out shears.*) Items on Bonaparte, for the press book. (*She turns and begins to unfold and clip a sheet of news-paper. JOE is at a loss for words.*)

JOE. (*Finally.*) Congratulations. . . .

LORNA. (*Without turning.*) Thanks. . . . (*In a sudden irresistible surge JOE tears papers out of LORNA'S hands and hurls them behind desk. The two stand facing each other.*)

JOE. When I speak to you, look at me!

LORNA. What would you like to say? (*They stand face to face, straining. Finally:*)

JOE. Marry anyone you like!

LORNA. Thanks for permission!

JOE. Queen Lorna, the tramp of Newark!

LORNA. You haven't spoken to me for months. Why break your silence?

JOE. You're a historical character for me—dead and buried!

LORNA. Then everything's simple; go about your business.

JOE. Moody's right for you—perfect—the mating of zero and zero!

LORNA. I'm not sorry to marry Tom ——

JOE. (*Scornfully.*) That's from the etiquette book—page twelve: " When you marry a man say you like it! "

LORNA. I know I could do worse when I look at you. When did you look in the mirror last? Getting to be a killer! You're getting to be like Fuseli! You're not the boy I cared about, not you. You murdered that boy with the generous face—God knows where you hid the body! I don't know you.

JOE. I suppose I never kissed your mouth ——

LORNA. What do you want from me? Revenge? Sorry—we're all out of revenge today!

JOE. I wouldn't look at you twice if they hung you naked from a Christmas tree! (*At this moment EDDIE FUSELI enters with a pair of packages. He looks intently at LORNA, then crosses and puts packages on desk. He and JOE are dressed almost identically. LORNA exits without a word. EDDIE is aware of what has happened but begins to talk casually about the packages.*)

EDDIE. This one's your new headgear. This is shirts from Jacobs Brothers. He says the neck bands are gonna shrink, so I had him make sixteens—they'll fit you after one washing. (*Holding up a shirt.*) You like that color?

JOE. Thanks.

EDDIE. Your brother-in-law drove me over. Picked him up on 49th. Don't you ever see them no more?

JOE. (*Sharply.*) What for?

EDDIE. What'sa matter?

JOE. Why? You see a crowd around here, Eddie?

EDDIE. No.

JOE. That's right, you don't! But I do! I see a crowd of Eddies all around me, suffocating me, burying me in good times and silk shirts!

EDDIE. (*Dialing phone.*) You wanna go to the Scandals tonight? I got tickets. (*Into telephone.*) Charley? Fuseli is speaking. . . . I'm giving four to five on Bonaparte tomorrow. . . . Four G's worth. . . . Yes. (*Hanging up phone.*) It's gonna be a good fight tomorrow.

JOE. (*Belligerently.*) How do you know?

EDDIE. I know Bonaparte. I got eighteen thousand spread out on him tomorrow night.

JOE. Suppose Bonaparte loses?

EDDIE. I look at the proposition from all sides—I know he'll win.

JOE. What the hell do you think I am? A machine? Maybe I'm lonely, maybe ——

EDDIE. You wanna walk in a parade? Everybody's lonely. Get the money and you're not so lonely.

JOE. I want some personal life.

EDDIE. I give Bonaparte a good personal life. I got loyalty to his cause. . . .

JOE. You use me like a gun! Your loyalty's to keep me oiled and polished!

EDDIE. A year ago Bonaparte was a rookie with a two-pants suit. Now he wears the best, eats the best, sleeps the best. He walks down the street respected—the golden boy! They howl their heads off when Bonaparte steps in the ring . . . and I done it for him!

JOE. There are other things. . . .

EDDIE. There's no other things! Don't think so much—it could make you very sick! You're in this up to your neck. You owe me a lot—I don't like you to forget. You better be on your toes when you step in that ring tomorrow night. (EDDIE *turns and begins to dial phone.*)

JOE. Your loyalty makes me shiver. (JOE *starts for door.*)

EDDIE. Take the shirts.

JOE. What do I want them for? I can only wear one at a time. . . . (EDDIE *speaks into phone.*)

EDDIE. Meyer? . . . Fuseli is speaking. . . . I'm giving four to five on Bonaparte tomorrow. . . . Two? . . . Yeah. . . . (*About to exit,* JOE *stands at the door and watches* EDDIE *as he calmly begins to dial phone again.*)

MEDIUM FADEOUT

ACT III

SCENE 2

The next night.

The lights fade in on an empty stage. We are in the same dressing room as seen in Act II, Scene 4. Far in the distance is heard the same roar of THE CROWD. *The distant bell clangs menacingly. The room is shadows and patches of light. The silence here has its own ugly dead quality.*

LORNA MOON *enters. She looks around nervously, she lights a cigarette, this reminds her to rouge her lips, she puffs the cigarette. The distant bell clangs again.* EDDIE FUSELI *enters, pale and tense. He sees* LORNA *and stops short in his tracks. There is an intense silence as they look at each other.*

LORNA. How's the fight?

EDDIE. I like to talk to you.

LORNA. Is Joe still on his feet?

EDDIE. Take a month in the country, Miss Moon.

LORNA. Why?

EDDIE. (*Repressing a murderous mood.*) Give the boy . . . or move away.

LORNA. I get married tomorrow. . . .

EDDIE. You heard my request—give him or go!

LORNA. Don't Moody count?

EDDIE. If not for Bonaparte they'd find you in a barrel long ago—in the river or a bush!

LORNA. I'm not afraid of you. . . . (*The distant bell clangs.*)

EDDIE. (*After turning his head and listening.*) That's the beginning of the eighth. Bonaparte's unsettled—fighting like a drunken sailor. He can't win no more, unless he knocks the Chocolate out. . . .

LORNA. (*At a complete loss.*) Don't look at me . . . what'd you . . . I . . .

EDDIE. Get outa town! (*The roar of* THE CROWD *mounts to a demand for a kill.* EDDIE, *listening intently.*) He's like a bum to-night . . . and a bum done it! You! (*The roar grows fuller.*) I can't watch him get slaughtered. . . .

LORNA. I couldn't watch it myself. (*The bell clangs loudly several times. The roar of* THE CROWD *hangs high in the air.*) What's happening now?

EDDIE. Someone's getting murdered. . . .

LORNA. It's me. . . .

EDDIE. (*Quietly, intensely.*) That's right . . . if he lost . . . the trees are ready for your coffin. (*The roar of* THE CROWD *tones down.*) You can go now. I don't wanna make a scandal around his name. . . . I'll find you when I want you. Don't be here when they carry him in.

LORNA. (*At a complete loss.*) Where do you want me to go?

EDDIE. (*Suddenly releasing his wrath.*) Get outa my sight! You turned down the sweetest boy who ever walked in shoes! You turned him down, the golden boy, that king among the ju-ven-iles! He gave you his hand—you spit in his face! You led him on like Gertie's whoore! You sold him down the river! And now you got the nerve to stand here, to wait and see him bleeding from the mouth! ——

LORNA. Fuseli, for God's sake ——

EDDIE. Get outa my sight!

LORNA. Fuseli, please ——

EDDIE. Outa my sight, you nickel whoore! (*Completely enraged and out of control,* EDDIE *half brings his gun out from under his left armpit.* JOE *appears in doorway. Behind him are* ROXY, MOODY *and a* SECOND.)

JOE. Eddie! (EDDIE *whirls around. The others enter the room. In* the ensuing silence, MOODY, sensing what has happened, crosses to LORNA.)

LORNA. (Quietly.) What happened?

ROXY. What happened? (He darts forward and picks up JOE'S arm in the sign of victory. The arm drops back limply.) The monarch of the masses!

EDDIE. (To the SECOND.) Keep everybody out. Only the news-paper boys. (The SECOND exits and closes the door. JOE sits on a table. Physically he is a very tired boy. There is a high puff under one eye, the other is completely closed. His body is stained with angry splotches.)

TOKIO. (Gently.) I have to hand it to you, Joe. . . .

ROXY. (Explaining to the frigid EDDIE, elaborately.) The beginning of the eighth: first the bell! Next the Chocolate Drop comes out like a waltz clog, confident. Oh, he was so confident! Haha! The next thing I know the Chocolate's on the floor, the referee lifts our arm, we got on our bathrobe and we're here in the dressing room! How do you like it?

EDDIE. (Narrowly.) I like it.

TOKIO. (Taking off JOE'S gloves.) I'll have you feelin' better in a minute. (After which he cuts the tapes.)

JOE. I feel all right.

EDDIE. (To TOKIO.) Gimme his gloves.

MOODY. (Wary of JOE.) That's a bad lump under your eye.

JOE. Not as bad as the Chocolate Drop got when he hit the floor!

ROXY. Darling, how you gave it to him! Not to my enemies!

JOE. 'Twas a straight right—with no trimmings or apologies! Aside from fouling me in the second and fifth ——

MOODY. I called them on it ——

ROXY. I seen the bastard ——

JOE. That second time I nearly went through the floor. I gave him the fury of a lifetime in that final punch! (EDDIE has taken the soggy boxing gloves for his own property. TOKIO is daubing the bruise under JOE'S eye.) And did you hear them cheer! (Bitterly, as if reading a news report.) Flash! As thousands cheer, that veritable whirlwind Bonaparte—that veritable cock-eye wonder, Bonaparte—he comes from behind in the eighth stanza to slaughter the Chocolate Drop and clinch a bout with the champ! Well, how do you like me, boys? Am I good or am I good?

ROXY. Believe me!

TOKIO. (*Attempting to settle* JOE.) You won the right for a crack at the title. You won it fair and clean. Now lay down. . . .

JOE. (*In a vehement outburst.*) I'd like to go outside my weight and beat up the whole damn world!

MOODY. (*Coldly.*) Well, the world's your oyster now!

TOKIO. (*Insistently.*) Take it easy. Lemme fix that eye, Joe —— (*Now a bustling little Irishman,* DRISCOLL, *hustles into the room.*)

DRISCOLL. Who's got the happy boy's gloves?

EDDIE. Here . . . why? (DRISCOLL *rapidly takes gloves, " breaks " and examines them.*)

TOKIO. What's the matter, " Drisc " ?

JOE. What's wrong?

DRISCOLL. (*Handing the gloves back to* EDDIE.) Chocolate's a sick boy. Your hands are clean. (DRISCOLL *hustles for the door.* JOE *is up and to him.*)

JOE. What happened?

DRISCOLL. (*Bustling.*) It looks like the Pride of Baltimore is out for good. Change your clothes.

JOE. How do you mean?

DRISCOLL. Just like I said—out! (DRISCOLL *pats* JOE'S *shoulder, hustles out, closing door in* JOE'S *face.* JOE *slowly sits on the nearest bench. Immediately* TOKIO *comes to him, as tender as a mother.*)

TOKIO. You didn't foul him—you're a clean fighter. You're so honest in the ring it's stupid. If something's happened, it's an accident. (*The others stand around stunned, not knowing what to do or say.*)

MOODY. (*Very worried.*) That's right, there's nothing to worry about.

ROXY. (*Ditto.*) That's right. . . .

JOE. Gee. . . . (JOE *stands up, slowly crosses the room and sits on the table, head in his hands, his back to the others. No one knows what to say.*)

EDDIE. (*To* MOODY.) Go out there and size up the situation.

(MOODY, *glad of the opportunity to leave the room, turns to the door which is suddenly violently thrust open.* BARKER, *the* CHOCO-LATE DROP'S *manager, pushes* MOODY *into the room with him, leaving door open. From outside a small group of curious people look in.* BARKER, *bereft of his senses, grabs* MOODY *by the coat lapel.*)

BARKER. Do you know it? Do you know it?

MOODY. Now wait a minute, Barker —— (BARKER *runs over to* JOE *and screams:*)

BARKER. You murdered my boy! He's dead! You killed him!

TOKIO. (*Getting between* JOE *and* BARKER.) Just a minute!

BARKER. (*Literally wringing his hands.*) He's dead! Chocolate's dead!

TOKIO. We're very sorry about it. Now pull yourself together.

(EDDIE *crosses room and slams door shut as* BARKER *points an accusing finger at* JOE *and screams:*)

BARKER. This dirty little wop killed my boy!

EDDIE. (*Coming to* BARKER.) Go back in your room.

BARKER. Yes, he did!! (EDDIE'S *answer is to shove* BARKER *roughly toward door, weeping.*) Yes, he did!!

EDDIE. Get out before I slug your teeth apart!

JOE. (*Jumping to his feet.*) Eddie, for God sakes, don't hit him! Let him alone! (EDDIE *immediately desists.* BARKER *stands there, a weeping idiot.*)

MOODY. Accidents can happen.

BARKER. I know . . . . know. . . .

MOODY. Chocolate fouled us twice.

BARKER. I know, I know. . . . (BARKER *stammers, gulps and tries to say something more. Suddenly he dashes out of the room. There is a long silent pause during which* JOE *sits down again.*)

EDDIE. We'll have to wait for an investigation.

TOKIO. (*To* JOE.) Don't blame yourself for nothing. . . .

JOE. That poor guy . . . with those sleepy little eyes. . . .

ROXY. (*Solemnly.*) It's in the hands of God, a thing like that.

(LEWIS, *the sports writer, tries to enter the room.*)

EDDIE. (*Herding him out.*) Stay outside. (*To* MOODY.) See what's happening? (MOODY *immediately leaves.*) Everybody out—-leave Bonaparte to calm hisself. I'll watch the door.

TOKIO. Don't worry, Joe. (*He exits, followed by* ROXY. EDDIE *turns and looks at* LORNA.)

EDDIE. You too, Miss Moon—this ain't no cocktail lounge.

LORNA. I'll stay here. (EDDIE *looks at her sharply, shifts his glance from her to* JOE *and back again, he exits.*) Joe. . . .

JOE. Gee, that poor boy. . . .

LORNA. (*Holding herself off.*) But it wasn't your fault.

JOE. That's right—it wasn't my fault!

LORNA. You didn't mean it!

JOE. That's right—I didn't mean it! I wouldn't want to do that, would I? Everybody knows I wouldn't want to kill a man. Lorna, you know it!

LORNA. Of course!

JOE. But I *did* it! That's the thing—I *did* it! What will my father say when he hears I murdered a man? Lorna, I see what I did. I murdered myself, too! I've been running around in circles. Now I'm smashed! That's the truth. Yes, I was a real sparrow, and I wanted to be a fake eagle! But now I'm hung up by my finger tips—I'm no good—my feet are off the earth!

LORNA. (*In a sudden burst, going to* JOE.) Joe, I love you! We love each other. Need each other!

JOE. Lorna darling, I see what's happened!

LORNA. You wanted to conquer the world ——

JOE. Yes ——

LORNA. But it's not the kings and dictators who do it—it's that kid in the park ——

JOE. Yes, that boy who might have said, " I have myself; I am what I want to be! "

LORNA. And now, tonight, here, this minute—finding yourself again—that's what makes you a champ. Don't you see that?

JOE. Yes, Lorna—yes!

LORNA. It isn't too late to tell the world good evening again!

JOE. With what? These fists?

LORNA. Give up the fighting business!

JOE. Tonight!

LORNA. Yes, and go back to your music ——

JOE. But my hands are ruined. I'll never play again! What's left, Lorna? Half a man, nothing, useless. . . .

LORNA. No, *we're* left! Two together! We have each other! Somewhere there must be happy boys and girls who can teach us the way of life! We'll find some city where poverty's no shame— where music is no crime!—where there's no war in the streets— where a man is glad to be himself, to live and make his woman herself!

JOE. No more fighting, but where do we go?

LORNA. Tonight? Joe, we ride in your car. We speed through the night, across the park, over the Triboro Bridge ——
JOE. (*Taking* LORNA'S *arms in his trembling hands.*) Ride! That's it, we ride—clear my head. We'll drive through the night. When you mow down the night with headlights, nobody gets you! You're on top of the world then—nobody laughs! That's it—speed! We're off the earth—unconnected! We don't have to think!! That's what speed's for, an easy way to live! Lorna darling, we'll burn up the night! (*He turns and as he begins to throw his street clothes out of his locker.*)

MEDIUM FADEOUT

ACT III

SCENE 3

Late the same night.
In the Bonaparte home, same as Act I, Scene 2, sit EDDIE FUSELI, MOODY, ROXY *and* SIGGIE, *drinking home-made wine, already half drunk.* BONAPARTE *stands on the other side of the room, looking out of the window.* FRANK *sits near him, a bandage around his head.* MOODY *is at telephone as the lights fade in.*

MOODY. (*Impatiently.*) . . . 'lo? Hello! . . .
SIGGIE. I'll tell you why we need another drink. . . .
ROXY. No, I'll tell you. . . .
MOODY. (*Turning.*) Quiet! For Pete's sake! I can't hear myself think! (*Turning to phone.*) Hello? . . . This is Moody. Any calls for me? Messages? . . . No sign of Miss Moon? . . . Thanks. Call me if she comes in—the number I gave you before. (*Hanging up and returning to his wine glass, to* BONAPARTE.) I thought you said Joe was coming up here!
BONAPARTE. I say maybe. . . .
MOODY. (*Sitting.*) I'll wait another fifteen minutes. (*He drinks.*)
SIGGIE. Here's why we need another drink; it's a night of success! Joe's in those lofty brackets from now on! We're gonna move to a better neighborhood, have a buncha kids! (*To* BONAPARTE.)

76

Hey, pop, I wish we had a mortgage so we could pay it off! To the next champ of the world! (SIGGIE *lifts his glass, the others join him.*)

ROXY. Bonaparte.

EDDIE. Don't you drink, Mr. Bonaparte?

SIGGIE. You, too, Frank—it's all in the family. (BONAPARTE *shrugs and comes down, accepting a glass.*)

ROXY. It's in the nature of a celebration!

BONAPARTE. My son'sa kill a man tonight—what'sa celebrate? What'sa gonna be, heh?

SIGGIE. Ahh, don't worry—they can't do him nothing for that! An accident!

EDDIE. (*Coldly, to* BONAPARTE.) Listen, it's old news. It's been out on the front page two-three hours.

BONAPARTE. Poor color' boy . . .

MOODY. Nobody's fault. Everybody's sorry—we give the mother a few bucks. But we got the next champ! Bottoms up. (*All drink,* FRANK *included.*)

ROXY. (*To* BONAPARTE.) You see how a boy can make a success nowadays?

BONAPARTE. Yeah . . . I see.

EDDIE. (*Resenting* BONAPARTE'S *attitude.*) Do we bother you? If I didn't think Joe was here I don't come up. I don't like nobody to gimme a boycott!

BONAPARTE. (*Going back to window.*) Helpa you'self to more wine.

SIGGIE. (*To* EDDIE.) Leave him alone—he don't feel social tonight.

MOODY. Don't worry, Mr. Bonaparte. Looka me—take a lesson from me—I'm not worried. I'm getting married tomorrow—*this afternoon!*—I don't know where my girl is, but I'm not worried! What for? We're all in clover up to our necks!

SIGGIE. Shh . . . don't wake up my wife. (MOODY *suddenly sits heavily, jealousy begins to gnaw at him despite his optimism.* ROXY *takes another drink.* EDDIE *asks* FRANK, *apropos of his bandaged head:*)

EDDIE. What's that " Spirit of '76 " outfit for?

SIGGIE. (*Grinning to* EDDIE.) Didn't you hear what he said before? They gave it to him in a strike ——

EDDIE. (*To* FRANK.) You got a good build—you could be a fighter.

FRANK. I fight. . . .

EDDIE. Yeah? For what?

FRANK. A lotta things I believe in. . . . .(EDDIE *looks at* FRANK *and appreciates his quality.*)

EDDIE. Whatta you get for it?

ROXY. (*Laughing.*) Can't you see? A busted head!

FRANK. I'm not fooled by a lotta things Joe's fooled by. I don't get autos and custom-made suits. But I get what Joe don't.

EDDIE. What don't he get? (BONAPARTE *comes in and listens intently.*)

FRANK. (*Modestly.*) The pleasure of acting as you think! The satisfaction of staying where you belong, being what you are . . . at harmony with millions of others!

ROXY. (*Pricking up his ears.*) Harmony? That's music! The family's starting up music again!

FRANK. (*Smiling.*) That's right, that's music —— (*Now* MOODY *emphatically stamps his glass down on table and stands.*)

MOODY. What's the use waiting around! They won't be back. (*Bitterly.*) Lorna's got a helluva lotta nerve, riding around in Long Island with him! Without even asking me!

SIGGIE. Long Island's famous for the best eating ducks.

EDDIE. (*To* MOODY.) You got the champ—you can't have everything.

MOODY. What's that supposed to mean?

EDDIE. (*Coldly.*) That girl belongs to Bonaparte. They're together now, in some roadhouse . . . and they ain't eating duck!

MOODY. (*Finally, unsteadily.*) You don't know what you're talking about!

EDDIE. Moody, what do you figger your interest is worth in Bonaparte?

MOODY. Why?

EDDIE. (*Without turning.*) Roxy . . . are you listening?

ROXY. Yeah. . . .

EDDIE. 'Cause after tonight I'd like to handle Bonaparte myself.

MOODY. . . . Your gall is gorgeous! But I got a contract. . . .

ROXY. Eddie, have a heart—I'm holding a little twenty percent.

(*Out of sheer rage* MOODY *drinks more wine,* ROXY *follows his example.*)

FRANK. (*To* EDDIE.) How much does Joe own of himself?

EDDIE. Thirty percent. After tonight I own the rest.

78

MOODY. Oh, no! No, sir-ee!!

EDDIE. You're drunk tonight! Tomorrow!

BONAPARTE. (*Coming forward.*) Maybe Joe don't gonna fight no more, after tonight. . . .

EDDIE. Listen, you creep! Why don't you change your tune for a minute!

ROXY. (*To* BONAPARTE.) What're *you* worried about?

BONAPARTE. My boy usta coulda be great for all men. Whatta he got now, heh? Pardon me fora nota to feel so confident in Joe'sa future! Pardon me fora to be anxious. . . .

EDDIE. (*Standing up.*) I don't like this talk!

SIGGIE. Sit down, pop—you're rocking the boat! Shh! Shh! (*He slips out of the room.*)

ROXY. Does anyone here know what he's talking about?

FRANK. He's trying to say he's worried for Joe.

ROXY. But why? Why? Don't he realize his kid's worth a fortune from tonight on? (*After giving* EDDIE *a quick glance.*) Ain't he got brains enough to see two feet ahead? Tell him in Italian—he don't understand our language—this is a festive occasion! To Bonaparte, the Monarch of the Masses! (*Telephone rings.*)

MOODY. (*Triumphantly, to* EDDIE.) That's my hotel! You see, you were all wrong! That's Lorna! (*Speaking into telephone.*) Hello? . . . No. . . . (*Turning to* BONAPARTE.) It's for you. (MOODY *extends telephone in* BONAPARTE'S *direction, but the latter stands in his place, unable to move. After a few seconds* FRANK *sees this and briskly moves to telephone, taking it from* MOODY. *In the meantime* MOODY *has begun to address* EDDIE *with drunken eloquence. Wavering on his feet.*) There's a constitution in this country, Eddie Fuseli. Every man here enjoys life, liberty and the pursuit of happiness!

FRANK. (*Speaking into telephone.*) Yes? . . . No, this is his son.

(BONAPARTE *watches* FRANK *mutely as he listens at telephone.*)

MOODY. There's laws in this country, Fuseli!—*Contracts!* We live in a civilized world ——!

FRANK. (*Loudly, to the others.*) Keep quiet! (*Resumes listening.*) Yes . . . yes. . . .

ROXY. (*To* EDDIE.) And there's a God in heaven—don't forget it!

FRANK. (*On telephone.*) Say it again. . . . (*He listens.*) Yes. . . .

MOODY. (*To* EDDIE.) You're a killer! A man tries to do his best—but you're a killer! (FRANK *lowers telephone and comes down to the others.*)

FRANK. *You're all killers!* (BONAPARTE *advances a step toward* FRANK.)

BONAPARTE. Frank . . . is it . . . ?

FRANK. I don't know how to tell you, poppa. . . .

BONAPARTE. (*Hopefully.*) Yes . . . ?

FRANK. We'll have to go there ——

EDDIE. Go where?

FRANK. Both of them . . . they were killed in a crash ——

EDDIE. Who?! What?!

FRANK. They're waiting for identification—Long Island, Babylon.

EDDIE. (*Moving to* FRANK.) What are you handing me?! (EDDIE, *suddenly knowing the truth, stops in his tracks. Telephone operator signals for telephone to be replaced. The mechanical clicks* [1] *call*

    [1] Need not be actually heard by audience.

FRANK *to attention, he slowly replaces the instrument.*)

MOODY. I don't believe that! Do you hear me? I don't believe it ——

FRANK. What waste! . . .

MOODY. It's a goddam lie!!

BONAPARTE. What have-a you expect? . . .

MOODY. (*Suddenly weeping.*) Lorna! . . .

BONAPARTE. (*Standing, his head high.*) Joe. . . . Come, we bring-a him home . . . where he belong. . . .

SLOW FADEOUT

PROPERTY LIST

ACT I, SCENE 2

3 or 4 newspapers
2 bottles of beer and glasses
Watch
Violin case with violin inside

ACT I, SCENE 3

Cigarettes and matches
Large white Panama hat

ACT I, SCENE 5

Suitcase
Wine in bottle and glasses for wine
Newspapers
Men's clothes to pack in suitcase
Tea apron
A man's sweater
A man's slippers

ACT II, SCENE 1

Large bath towel
Small head towel

ACT II, SCENE 2

Man's handkerchief, used

ACT II, SCENE 3

Roll of paper money

ACT II, SCENE 4

Water pail
Extra pair of men's shoes
Bathrobe
Used boxing gloves
Sport shirt
Various articles of boxing para-
phernalia

ACT III, SCENE 1

Sandwich
Package of cigarettes and matches
Several newspapers
Pair of scissors
Paper clips
A pair of packages including new
shirts

ACT III, SCENE 2

Cigarettes and matches
A pair of boxing gloves with tapes
A small piece of absorbent cotton
Man's street clothes

ACT III, SCENE 3

Bottle of home-made wine and
glasses
Head bandage

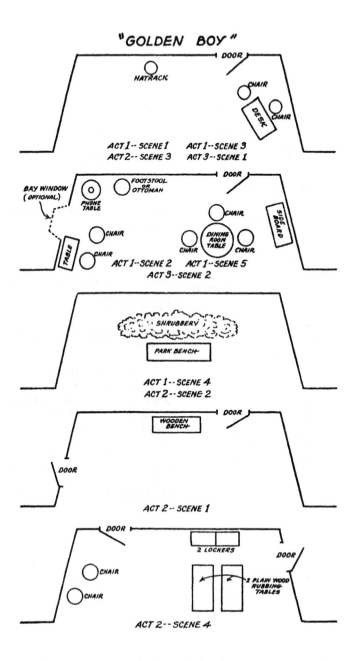

NOTES
(Use this space to make notes for your production)

NOTES
(Use this space to make notes for your production)

NOTES

(Use this space to make notes for your production)

NOTES
(Use this space to make notes for your production)